Them He Glorified

Them He Glorified

*A Systematic Study of
the Doctrine of Glorification*

by

BERNARD RAMM

*Professor of Systematic Theology
California Baptist Theological Seminary*

Wm. B. Eerdmans Publishing Company
Grand Rapids, Michigan

PHOTOLITHOPRINTED BY CUSHING - MALLOY, INC.
ANN ARBOR, MICHIGAN, UNITED STATES OF AMERICA
1963

PREFACE

In the years that I have taught doctrine or systematic theology I have found the students always surprised at the riches of the New Testament doctrine of glorification. Looking further into the subject matter, I found no book which systematically explored the doctrine. In books on salvation a few pages are usually given over to glorification and there is a spate of books on heaven. But I have found no work which begins with the eschatological character of our present salvation and follows its course to its fruition in the glorification of the believer. So I have undertaken the task myself. Briefly, the thesis of the book is that salvation is eschatological to the core. Therefore, present salvation is anticipatory of further salvation. The bringing to perfection of our present salvation in the future end-time is exactly the substance of the doctrine of glorification.

As I was writing this work, the name of A. L. Ritts, a dedicated lay Bible teacher, continually came before my consciousness because he was the first one to set before my believing eyes the glories of Jesus Christ and the believer's share in these glories.

—BERNARD RAMM

Seminary Knolls
Covina, California

CONTENTS

ABBREVIATIONS

EGT, *Expositors Greek Testament*

EKL, *Evangelisches Kirchen Lexikon*

HDB, *Hastings Dictionary of the Bible*

HERE, *Hastings Encyclopedia of Religion and Ethics*

ICC, *International Critical Commentary*

ISBE, *International Standard Bible Encyclopedia*

RGG (3), *Die Religion in Geschichte und Gegenwart,* third edition

TWNT, *Theologisches Wörterbuch zum Neuen Testament*

As for me, I cannot say that I will speak of the glory, but I will try to stammer about it; for the best language to which a man can reach concerning glory must be a mere stammering. —CHARLES SPURGEON, *Sermons,* 14:183-184

I The Glory of God in the Old Testament

SECTION 1: *The concept of glory*[1]

Glory is one of the great words of the English language. It is so rich in connotations that no single word can serve as a good synonym. It means honor, praise, splendor, radiance, pomp, power, exaltation, and supreme worthiness. In English usage it is one of the few words that can stand for all that the word *heaven* represents. In one of its most remarkable usages in the Old Testament it is a synonym for the true and living God in contrast to the *glory-less* gods of paganism (Jer. 2:11).

There are more than a dozen Hebrew words which were translated by the King James translators with the English word *glory*.[2] The most important of these is *kabod*. The original meaning of this Hebrew word, however, is so different from the English word that it requires some effort to distinguish the two. *Kabod* means, basically, heaviness or weight. The closest English word is *gravity*, which signifies both weight and importance. The Hebrew *kabod*, however, eventually picked up a connotation of splendor which is not present in the English word *gravity*. Added to the notion of weight is

1. For general discussions of glory (*kabod*) cf.: G. von Rad, *Theologie des Alten Testaments*, I, 238-240. Th. Vriezen, *An Outline of Old Testament Theology*, pp. 246f. E. Jacob, *Theology of the Old Testament*, pp. 79f. G. A. F. Knight, *A Christian Theology of the Old Testament*, pp. 95ff. L. Köhler, *Old Testament Theology*, pp. 124ff. A. Richardson, editor, *A Theological Word Book of the Bible*, pp. 175-176. R. Rendtorff, "Die Offenbarungsvorstellungen im Alten Israel," *Offenbarung als Geschichte*, pp. 28-32. G. H. Molin, "Herrlichkeit," *Bibeltheologisches Wörterbuch*, pp. 405-410. G. von Rad, *TWNT*, II, 236-255. G. Henton Davies, "Glory," *The Interpreter's Dictionary of the Bible*, II, 401-403.

2. Cf. Young, *Analytical Concordance*, under *glory*.

also the notion of number. The numerous soldiers of an army are the *kabod* of the nation, and the great number of trees in a forest is the *kabod* of the forest.

What *kabod* meant to the Hebrews can best be learned by examining how they used the word. Whatever possessed weight in the sense of dignity was called *kabod*. *Kabod* refers to that which is fundamentally perceptible or ostentatious. Thus it means splendor, show, honor, conspicuousness, and even beauty. A man's wealth, the insignia of his wealth, and the pomp of his surroundings were called his *kabod*.[3]

In other words, the over-all impression of a rich man with his garments, jewels, attendants, etc., is the rich man's *kabod*. Psalm 49:16 is illuminating in this connection. It speaks of the *kabod*, i.e., wealth, of the rich man. When he dies he cannot take his *kabod* with him! Psalm 24:7-10 speaks of God as The King of Glory, i.e., as the God who reigns as a king surrounded by the pomp, splendor, beauty, and attendants which symbolize the king's court. Besides rich men and kings, *kabod* is attributed to things, e.g., to a temple, a throne, a crown, a chariot, a city, and a kingdom. In each instance *kabod* carries the ideas of importance, weight, honor, brilliance, splendor and fame.

It was not therefore difficult for the Hebrew mind to use *kabod* with reference to God. Here we rise analogically from the *kabod* of men and things to the *kabod* of God.[4] God possesses weight, gravity, honor, fame, dignity, and splendor, hence he is a God of *kabod*. This attribution of *kabod* to God is, as already noted in the reference to Jeremiah 2:11, one of the unique elements in the biblical revelation of God. *Kabod* is both a modality of the self-revelation of God, and an attribute of God.

The use of *kabod* is not uniform in the Old Testament canon

3. Instructive is the antonym for glory, *qlwn*, "shame, personal dishonor, disgrace, ignominy." Cf. "I will change their glory into shame" (Hos. 4:7). "And shame shall come upon your glory" (Hab. 2:16). Cf. Gall, *Die Herrlichkeit Gottes*, p. 5.

4. Cf. von Rad, *TWNT*, II, 241. In his *Theologie des Alten Testaments* von Rad notes that *kabod* is used in two ways with reference to God; first, as expressing his worth, power, and majesty; second, as a manifestation form of radiant light. *Op. cit.*, I, 238f.

but reveals different emphases by different authors. There was, however, a certain fixation of meaning which occurred when the Hebrew Testament was translated into the Greek language (the Septuagint). The principal Greek word used to translate the Hebrew *kabod* is *doxa.*

There is a double transformation at this point: one is in the meaning of the Greek word *doxa,* and the other is in the enrichment of the Hebrew concept of *kabod.* The ordinary meaning of the Greek *doxa* is opinion, or more specifically, the opinion which people have of other people, i.e., fame. In the Greek translation of the Old Testament, *doxa* acquires the meaning of glory.[5] Secondly, the word *doxa* is used to translate virtually all the Hebrew words for glory and this develops the term remarkably. The traditional meaning of the word in the classical literature drops out and is replaced by the rich Hebrew concept of the glory of God. Speaking of the use of *doxa* in the Greek translation Kittel says:

> The most important significance of this word in the Septuagint begins where it speaks about God. As with *kabod* it speaks properly of *God's honor* and *God's power.* The explanation about the particular occurrences of the word can only be a help, for already the concept speaks about the One. Thus *God's power* is an expression of his divine essence; *the honor,* which men acknowledge to him, is finally nothing less than the affirmation of this same essence. This *divine glory,* which reveals his essence in his creation and in his deeds, which fills the earth and the heavens, is called the *doxa theou* [glory of God]. Even so the *divine form of manifestation* and the *form of revelation* of the *kabod,* as it dominates certain parts of the Old Testament, is for the translator the becoming visible,, the self-revelation of this essence. Therefore this *divine radiance* in the giving of the law, in the tabernacle, in the temple is correctly translated by *doxa.* As the sign of this *divine essence* in its invisible or visibly perceptible form has the *doxa* of the

5. The transition of the word *doxa* from opinion to glory is a complex one and the subject of much scholarly research. The fundamental literature is cited in Arndt and Gingrich, *A Greek English Lexicon to the New Testament, under doxa;* in Harrison, "Glory," *Dictionary of Theology,* p. 237; and in A. M. Ramsay, *The Glory of God and the Transfiguration of Christ,* Chapter II, "The History of a Word."

Septuagint (and with it the biblical terminology) preserved its authentic expression.[6]

SECTION 2: *The glory of God as a form of the divine revelation*

God revealed himself to Israel by a number of modalities,[7] and his *kabod* is one of these. Hence Gall calls the glory of God "the revelatory glory of Yahwe."[8]

(1) The first reference to the glory as a form of the divine revelation is the pillar of fire and the cloud of the Exodus account. In the daytime the Israelites were led by the bright cloud and in the evening by the pillar of fire. This pillar was more than the providential means for directing the movements of the hosts of Israel, for it is identified with the presence of God (Exod. 14:23) and the glory of God (Exod. 16:10).

It appears, however, that the glory *per se* was not the cloud nor the fire but the fiery Presence within the pillar. For example, Exodus 24:17 says: "Now the appearance of the glory of the Lord was like a devouring fire on the top of the mountain in the sight of the people of Israel."[9] Along with the gleaming, darting, burning fire there were other manifestations. The glory was usually accompanied by meteorological phenomena such as *thunder* (cf. I Sam. 7:10, 12:17, 18, Exod. 20:18, Ps. 77:18), *lightning* (cf. II Sam. 22:15, Ezek. 1:13, 14, Exod. 19:16), and *clouds.* The luminous cloud is the most important of the three phenomena.[10] The account of Sinai given in Hebrews 12:18-19 lists a burning fire, darkness, gloom, storms or whirlwinds, a trumpet sound, and a sound caused by a spoken word. As Lang has said,

6. *TWNT,* II, 247-248.
7. I have attempted to spell these out in *Special Revelation and the Word of God,* Division II.
8. "Offenbarungsherrlichkeit Jahwes," *op. cit.,* p. 17.
9. Thus F. Hesse calls the glory here a "streaming, fiery substance," *RGG* (3), III, 273. The very intimate connection between fire and the divine presence is seen in Daniel 7:9-10 ("his throne was fiery flames, its wheels were burning fire. A stream of fire issued and came forth from before him").
10. Cf. *nephelē, TWNT,* IV, 904-912.

In almost all of the theophanies of the Old Testament fire appears as the form of representation of the unapproachable holiness and overpowering glory of Yahweh. Fundamental for the later representations was the manifestation of God on Mt. Sinai (Exodus 19) with various lines directed towards weather with lightning and thunder, and upon volcanic eruption associated with earthquake.[11]

(2) We note, next, that God revealed himself to Israel by his glorious presence in the tabernacle. According to Exodus 25:8, God instructed Moses as follows: "And let them make me a sanctuary, that I may dwell (*shakan*) in their midst." When the tabernacle was finished, the glory of the Lord came down and filled it (Exod. 40:34). Thus the dwelling of God among his people is specifically signified by the dwelling of his glory in the tabernacle, as it was later in the temple. The rabbinical expression "shekinah glory" reflects this teaching.[12] In the Epistle to the Romans (9:4) the apostle Paul affirmed that this manifestation of the divine presence was one of Israel's greatest benefits, for he wrote that to them belonged the *glory*. Similarly, the cherubim of the mercy seat are called (in Heb. 9:5) "cherubim of glory" because of the glory that glowed between them.

The dwelling of the glory of God in the tabernacle not only

---

11. *TWNT*, VI, 934. Cf. Deut. 5:23-26: "And when you heard the voice out of the midst of the darkness, while the mountain was burning with fire, you came near to me, all the heads of your tribes, and your elders; and you said, 'Behold, the Lord our God has shown us his glory and greatness, and we have heard his voice out of the midst of the fire; we have this day seen God speak with man and man still live. Now therefore why should we die? For this great fire will consume us . . . . For who is there of all flesh, that has heard the voice of the living God speaking out of the midst of fire, as we have, and has still lived?' "

12. Cf. J. J. Price, "Shekinah," *HERE*, XI, 450-452; *TWNT*, II, 248-250. "The Shekinah was the visible majesty of the divine presence, especially when dwelling between the cherubim in the tabernacle and Temple in the midst of God's people Israel" *The Westminster Dictionary of the Bible*. U. Simon, *Heaven in the Christian Tradition*, p. 83ff. The other side of this concept is that the visiting worshipper to the temple sits (*shakan*) in the courtyard of the temple to worship the Lord and be blessed by him. Cf. Pedersen, *Israel*, III-IV, p. 451. Ramsay notes that the shekinah was not used by the rabbis directly to indicate the glory of God but was used as a euphemism for the presence of God. *Op. cit.*, p. 18ff.

gives a visible sign of the presence of the Lord but it also makes the entire structure holy. This is seen in the events of Leviticus 10, where Nadab and Abihu offered strange or unholy fire before the Lord. The exact nature of the infraction cannot be deciphered from the text, but it is certain that the tabernacle was holy because of the shekinah glory. Upon the death of the two sons of Aaron, Moses says to Aaron, "This is what the Lord has said, 'I will show myself holy among those who are near me, and before all the people I will be glorified'" (Lev. 10:3 and Exod. 14:4, 17).

At the dedication of the temple, which was the successor to the tabernacle, the glory of the Lord filled the temple just as it filled the tabernacle at its completion. "And when the priests came out of the holy place, a cloud filled the house of the Lord, so that the priests could not stand to minister because of the cloud; for the glory of the Lord filled the house of the Lord" (I Kings 8:10-11, II Chron. 5:13-14, 7:1-3).

Finally, we have the departure of the shekinah glory from the temple and the city as recounted by Ezekiel.[13] The glory first moves to the threshold of the house, filling the courtyard with its brightness (10:4). Next, the glory moves to the east gate of the temple (10:19), and finally the glory moves to the traditional spot of the Mount of Olives (11:22-25).

It is at this spot that Zechariah (14:4) locates the manifestation of the Lord in messianic times. Some commentators see in the incarnation of Christ the return of the shekinah glory and the realization of its great intention (John 1:14). In this connection Simon writes:

> On the contrary: the glory-kabod of the Bible, the glory-yeqarah of the Aramaic Targums, the Doxa of the Greek Septuagint, converge upon the figure of Jesus, the focal point of the divine Presence who fulfils the expectation of God's visitation. This is the first complete departure from Rabbinic and Hellenistic Judaism, and from Gnostic sources of light mysticism.[14]

13. For an attempt to correlate this departure of the glory with the departure theme of the gods cf. H. G. May, "The Departure of the Glory of Yahweh," *Journal of Biblical Literature*, 56:309-321, 1937.

14. *Op. cit.*, p. 85. The Jewish expectations are expressed in the following: "The World to Come is not like this world. In the World to

(3) In the visions of Ezekiel we have yet more Old Testament materials on the glory of the Lord. Ezekiel speaks of seeing visions of God (1:1), and the vision that follows is very complex. There are the typical weather phenomena (stormy wind, great cloud, fire, thunder) and along with these are living creatures who have a fundamentally human form (1:5) but with four faces and four wings.

The center of interest, however, is not in the fearsome weather phenomena nor in the fast-moving living creatures, but in the theophany of the Lord. At the center of the phenomena was something which looked like burning coals of fire, like torches moving to and fro (v. 13). In verse 4 it is likened to gleaming bronze. Around this fiery something was a symbolization of the court of heaven: the firmament shining like crystal, the likeness of a throne, burning fire, and a rainbow.

The one seated on the throne has a human form (1:26), and this central figure Ezekiel calls "the appearance of the likeness of the glory of the Lord" (1:28). The glory of God is not in the weather phenomena, nor in the living creatures, nor in the accoutrements of the heavenly throne. It is in the gleaming, burning, fiery human form upon the crystal throne which is in the center of the theophany.[15] Here for the first time in the biblical record there is the union of the glory of God and the human form. The vision of Isaiah 6;1ff.) is more general than that of Ezekiel,[16] and that of Daniel (7:9ff.) is more particular.

Another special feature of this manifestation of the glory of the Lord is that it occurred in a private vision, unlike

---

come there is no eating and drinking, no begetting of children, no bargaining, no jealousy and hatred, and no strife; but the righteous sit with their crowns on their heads enjoying the effulgence of the Presence (Skekinah)." *Bab. Berakot* 17a, cited by S. Mowinckel, *He That Cometh*, p. 279.

15. Cf. *TWNT*, II, 244. *ISBE*, II, 1237. Gall, *op. cit.*, p. 29.

16. Zimmerli notes that Ezekiel, unlike Isaiah, does not fall down due to a sense of sin but is overcome by the divine majesty. W. Zimmerli, *Ezechiel (Biblischer Kommentar für Altes Testament)*, p. 57. He also notes that the glory of God in Ezekiel is not an attribute but "the personal presence of Yahweh in his glorious manifestation in light." P. 58.

the more public visions of the Pentateuch.[17]   In addition, the glory of God is localized upon an exalted, heavenly throne. Certainly Ezekiel's vision of the glory of God is one of the most stirring and graphic in the entire Scripture.

(4) The prophets also saw the glory of God in connection with creation. The profound creation-faith of Israel has only recently come into proper focus. It is almost unanimously agreed that the Bible-and-science controversy obscured the biblical doctrine of creation rather than illuminated it; and it is almost unanimously agreed that Israel first learned of the Lord as Redeemer, and then as Creator. In the Old Testament text the creation account comes before the redemption from Egypt, but the order of Israel's experience was the reverse. Through the grace and love of election and through the power of the redemption from Egypt, Israel came to know the Lord as Redeemer. Then, having learned that the Lord was Redeemer, Israel came to know the Lord as Creator. This holds true also for Psalm 19. In this Psalm the knowledge of the glory of God in the heavens precedes the knowledge of God in the Law; but the order of experience was the reverse.[18]

A second important consideration for understanding the glory of God in the creation of the world is that the Hebrews had no formulated doctrine of secondary causes. God's touch upon creation was direct; God's action upon man or nature was always an imminent possibility. Hence the usual battery of philosophical entities erected between God and his creation is totally absent from the biblical perspective.

The God of the Hebrews is a powerful, majestic, and glorious God. Whatever he does is an expression of his power, majesty, and glory. Creation is a manifestation of God's activity and

17. Cf. *TWNT*, II, 243-244.
18. Cf. G. C. Berkouwer, "The Nature Psalms," in *General Revelation*, pp. 117-134. G. S. Gunn, "The Fringes of His Ways," *God in the Psalms*, pp. 31-52. *TWNT*, III, 1004f. Von Rad said that Israel's connection of creation with *Heilsgeschichte* and not with myth "was a great theological achievement." *Theologie*, I, 141. Vriezen writes that "this linking together of Israel's faith in the God of Salvation with the Creation of the world gives to the Old Testament philosophy of life a clarity, tranquility, warmth, and grandeur not to be found outside the Bible." *An Outline of Old Testament Theology*, p. 186. His discussion begins at page 183.

therefore it is a manifestation of the glory of God.   In this connection we have the famous nature Psalms (8, 19, 29, 65, 105, 126, 147), the most unusual of which is Psalm 19:

> The heavens are telling the glory of God;
>   and the firmament proclaims his handiwork.
> Day to day pours forth speech,
>   and night to night declares knowledge.
> There is no speech, nor are there words;
>   their voice is not heard;
> Yet their voice goes out through all the earth,
>   and their words to the end of the world.

These verses teach that: (i) the heavens are the direct creation of God and therefore are a reflection of his glory; (ii) this reflection is a continuous telling and proclaiming; (iii) the day in its brightness and the night in its beauty maintain a twenty-four hour witness;[19] and (iv) this is not a revelation in uttered speech[20] but a wordless proclamation. The telling and proclaiming (these are participles in the Hebrew, stressing the continuous character of the witness) is paralleled by a seeing in the believing Hebrew.   (v) It is a revelation of God to all men who see the brilliance of the sun and the beauty of the night, for each is a species of the revelation of the glory of God.

(5) The glory of God is also seen in his deeds.   Whatever God does he does out of the perfection of his being.   Creation as an outgoing of the being of God accordingly reflects the glory of God.   The same is true of the redeeming and judging works of God, for issuing out of his perfection they reflect his glory.   This is seen in different ways in the various Old Testament narratives.

In the contest of the Lord with Pharaoh there is a pitting of the sovereign God against a stubborn man.   The Lord wins the victory, and this is called an acquiring of glory to the Lord (Exod. 14:17-18).   Again, in his great Psalm recorded in I Chronicles 16:24 David parallels the "marvelous works of God" with "his glory."   According to Ezekiel 39:21, the

---

19. "The poet is impressed by the beauty of nature." Arthur Weiser, *Die Psalmen (Das Alte Testament Deutsch)*, p. 133.

20. The King James is in error in its translation of verse 3.

judgment which the Lord executes is the same as "setting my glory among the nations." Because of "all thy works" the saints shall "speak of thy glory" (Ps. 145:10-13), and in the same Psalm the "mighty deeds" of the Lord are "the glorious splendor of thy kingdom" (v. 12). Speaking of the triumph of God in the exodus from Egypt, the prophetic word is given that "all the earth shall be filled with the glory of God" (Num. 14:21).

SECTION 3:   *The glory of God as an attribute of God*

In its original conception the glory of God is thought to be something perceptible. This perceptible element never becomes lost, but the idea of divine glory does become more abstract. The visible splendor, brilliance, and majesty of God become analogues for the invisible perfection of God. In more theological language, the glory of God as a form of the self-manifestation of God becomes spiritualized and is interpreted as a divine attribute.[21]

The glory of God is not, however, a particularized attribute like the wisdom of God but an attribute of the total nature of God, virtually an attribute of the attributes. Jacob says that "it is a kind of totality of qualities which make up his divine power."[22] God is glorious in his entire being. He is a being of such perfection and beauty that the word glory (*kabod*) serves as a synonym for God himself: "Has a nation changed its gods, even though they are no gods? But my people have changed their glory [i.e., their God] for that which does not profit" (Jer. 2:11).

Furthermore, only the Lord, not the pagan gods, possesses

21. In this connection compare the remark of A. R. Whitham: "The *doxa* of man, human opinion, etc., is shifting, uncertain, often based on error, and its pursuit for its own sake is unworthy. But there is a *doxa* with God which must be absolutely true and changeless. God's 'opinion' makes the true value of things, as they appear to the eternal mind; and God's 'favorable opinion' is true 'glory' . . . . Hence, 'glory' whether applied to God Himself or to His works as seen by Him, must imply the absolute truth which underlies all phenomena . . . the 'glory of God' therefore, must mean His essential and unchanging Godhead as revealed to man." "Glory," *Dictionary of Christ and the Gospels,* I, 648.

22. *Theology of the Old Testament,* p. 79.

glory. No lifeless god can partake of this glory, for it belongs to the living God! Therefore through the prophet Isaiah the Lord of glory says that "I am the Lord, that is my name; my glory I give to no other, nor my praise to graven images" (Isa. 42:8). On this point we may also consider Psalm 106: 19-20: "They made a calf in Horeb and worshipped a molten image. They exchanged the glory of God for the image of an ox that eats grass." The interesting parallel in this passage is between the *image* of the ox and the *glory* of God. The image is the form or pattern of the ox. To make such an image is to make a representation of God contrary to the Ten Commandments. That which represents God to the believing Israelite is the *glory* of God. Therefore that which the idolatrous image replaces in the true worship of God is the glory of God (cf. Rom. 1:23).

The totality-character of God's glory can also be seen in the manifold links which join it to his other attributes. It can be matched with holiness (Exod. 28:22, Isa. 6:3); with majesty, dignity, and splendor (Job 40:10); with majesty (Ps. 8:1, Isa. 35:1); and with power (Ps. 63:2). There is also an intimate relationship between the glory of God and light (Isa. 60:1-3), for the shining of the light of the Lord upon his people is synonymous with the rising of the glory of the Lord upon them.

If there is a bridge which connects the visible glory of the Lord with his essential being, it is that of the kingship.[23] The oriental king was surrounded by glory in the fundamental meaning of the word as indicating wealth, importance, honor, splendor and pomp. It might be said that the ancient oriental king personified glory. Therefore the royal kingship becomes one of the richest sources of analogies in the Old Testament for the doctrine of God. The *kabod* of the earthly king becomes the analogue for the *kabod* of the Lord. This is seen so clearly in Psalm 24:7-10:

> Lift up your heads, O gates!
>   and be lifted up, O ancient doors!
>   that the King of glory may come in.

23. Cf. *TWNT*, I, 566ff. (3. Yahwe als König).

Who is the King of glory?
The Lord, strong and mighty,
the Lord, mighty in battle!
Lift up your heads, O gates!
and be lifted up, O ancient doors!
that the King of glory may come in!
Who is this King of Glory?
The Lord of hosts,
he is the King of glory!

SECTION 4: *The glory of God and the beauty of God*

It is recorded in Exodus 33 that Moses made a request to
see the glory of the Lord (v. 18). The Lord replies that
He will show his glory to Moses under certain conditions. No
man can endure the face of the Lord and live (v. 20). Moses
may see the glory of the Lord only if hidden in a rock and only
as he sees its afterglow. In verse 19 the Lord says that he
will make his *tuv* pass before Moses. The word *tuv* in this
connection is used as a synonym for glory (*kabod*), the
Septuagint using *doxa* for both *kabod* and *tuv*.

There are some scholars who believe that *beauty* is the best
translation of *tuv* in this verse. Gall thinks that this is the
meaning here, for he finds *tuv* paralleled by beauty (*yphy*) in
Zechariah 9:17 and the *tuv*-neck of Hosea 10:11 can only
mean a beautiful neck.[24] Harrison thinks that "moral beauty"
is the best translation.[25] Von Rad[26] and Koehler-Baumgartner[27]
translate it with the German word *Schönheit* (beauty). Vos[28]
thinks that loveliness is a possible translation.

There are other suggestions of the association of beauty with
glory. The garments of the priests were for "glory and beauty"
(Exod. 28:2). God is to be worshipped in glorious garments

24. *Op. cit.,* p. 16.

25. "Glory," *Dictionary of Theology,* p. 236.

26. *TWNT,* II, 242.

27. *Lexikon in Veteris Testamenti Libros.* They cite also Hosea 10:11
and Zech. 9:17.

28. *Biblical Theology,* p. 120. Esther is described as beautiful (*tobat
mareh*), Esther 2:7. The same expression occurs in II Sam. 11:2. There
occurs in Song of Solomon 2:5 the very unusual expression: *the beauty
of his glory* (*to kallos tēs doxēs autou*).

(I Chron. 16:29). The Psalms speak of wanting to see the beauty of the Lord (Ps. 27:4). Isaiah speaks of the branch of the Lord being beautiful and glorious (28:5). In Isaiah 64:11 we have a beautiful and holy house; in 52:1, beautiful garments; and in 35:2 the beautiful landscape of Lebanon (the Switzerland of ancient Palestine) is called its glory. In conclusion there is one Hebrew word (tp'rth) which means both beauty and glory. In the King James version it is translated glory 22 times, glorious 3 times, and beautiful 6 times.

Stealing a look at the Greek *doxa* we note that there are instances when it, too, can possibly mean beauty. The woman's luxurious head of hair is called her beauty (*doxa*, I Cor. 11:15). The beauty of a flower is called *doxa* (I Pet. 1:24) and the beauty of the lily which is greater than the *kabod* of Solomon is called *doxa* (Matt. 5:29, Luke 12:27).

The history of theology presents us with an ambiguous chapter on the beauty of God. Augustine, in the neo-Platonic tradition, does not hestitate to call God beautiful. He calls God the Father of the beautiful[29] and also writes "for when the soul sees that unique and true Beauty it will love it more."[30]

One of the very few discussions of the beauty of God in systematic theology will be found in Karl Barth's *Church Dogmatics*.[31] In his exposition on the glory of God he says that not everything has been said about glory until something is said about the relationship of glory to beauty. The glory of God is such that it reveals God who is pleasant, desirable, and full of enjoyment. In knowing this God and desiring him, we find him beautiful. But the notion that God is beautiful is not a leading biblical notion but a secondary one. The primary focus of Scripture is on the glory of God as such, the aesthetic motif being purely secondary.

---

29. "Father of Truth, of Wisdom, of the True and Perfect life, of Beautitude, of the Good and Beautiful, of the Intelligible Light, Father of our awakening, and of our illumination of the sign by which we are admonished to return to thee." *Soliloquies*, I, 3.

30. *Ibid.*, 1, 13. In *Confessions*, I, 4, 4, he calls God "most beauteous," and in III, 6, 10 he calls God the "beauty of all things beautiful."

31. II/1, p. 650.

SECTION 5:   *The glory of God as something returned to God*

The glory of God is the excellence, beauty, majesty, power and perfection of his total being. It is the completeness, the wholeness, and therefore the utter desirability of God. It is the appeal, the fascinating power, the attraction which he exerts over men. The man so affected by the glory of God returns glory to him by praise and adoration. Thus glory is not only a totality—character of God but something which the creature returns to the Creator.

This returning of glory to God occurs at two kinds of occasions: (i) when man reflects in general upon the glory of God, the perfection of God, the greatness and majesty of God, he bursts forth with praise and adoration to this God; or, (ii) when man perceives the glory of God in one of the divine acts, he renders praise to God. Most relevant Scripture passages refer to the second of these. Thus glory is *rendered* to God (I Sam. 6:5, I Chron. 16:29), or *ascribed* to God (Ps. 29:1-2) or *given* to God (Mal. 2:2). Therefore the great achievement of the creature is that he enters into this glorification of God. "Thus says the Lord: 'Let not the wise man glory in his wisdom, let not the mighty man glory in his might, let not the rich man glory in his riches; but let him who glories glory in this, that he understands and knows me, that I am the Lord who practices kindness, justice, and righteousness in the earth; for in these things I delight, says the Lord'" (Jer. 9:23-24). And the man who so glorifies God can only concur with the Psalmist (115:1) when he writes: "Not to us, O Lord, not to us, but to thy name give glory."

SECTION 6:   *The glory of the Lord as an eschatological manifestation*

A remarkable aspect of the glory of God as revealed in the Old Testament is its eschatological outbreaking.[32]   This is taught primarily in the later chapters of Isaiah and Ezekiel, which deal with messianic expectations. The root of this

---

32. Cf. Gall, *op. cit.*, pp. 32, 26. Von Rad, *Theologie*, II, 305. An important summary of all the references is given in Brown, Driver and Briggs, *A Hebrew and English Lexicon of the Old Testament*, pp. 458-459.

doctrine is the expectation that some day the entire earth will be filled with the glory of the Lord (e.g., Num. 14:21, Ps. 72:19, Hab. 2:14). In this age, the now-age, the wonders of God are partial, not full; they are veiled, not manifest; the power of God is restricted, not fully expressed. But in some future day the glory of God shall break through these self-imposed limitations and the earth will be filled with the glory of the Lord.

This is distinctly a messianic expectation. But the data about the eschatological manifestation of the glory of the Lord cannot be systematically related. Neither is it possible to harmonize into a unified system all the messianic statements. In Psalm 72:19 it is the earth that is full of the glory of God; in Haggai 2:3-9 it is the "latter house"; in Ezekiel 43:2-5 it is the new temple. Isaiah says that all flesh shall see the glory of the Lord (40:5), and Zechariah says that the Lord will show his glory within the reconstructed Jerusalem and so will be a wall of fire around her.[33] Isaiah says that the Messianic Branch will be beautiful and glorious (11:10), that he will have a glorious throne (22:23), and that in messianic days the glory of the Lord will shine upon the earth (60:1-3).

33. Von Rad says that it was the condition of Israel which caused Zechariah to limit his prophecy of the future glory to the city. *Ibid.*, II, 305.

II The Glory of God in the New Testament

SECTION 7: *Old Testament connections*

The New Testament understanding of glory has its roots in the Old Testament teaching of the *kabod,* and moreover in the Septuagint teaching of *doxa.* When the New Testament uses *doxa* it is according to Septuagint usage and not classical.[1]

Many cases of the Old Testament *kabod* can be found in the New Testament. The kings live in their courts in luxury and are clothed with magnificent apparel. This is their glory (*endoxos,* Luke 7:25). Solomon was a king who lived in great glory (Matt. 6:29, Luke 12:28). In the book of Revelation the kings of the earth are represented as bringing their glory to the New Jerusalem (Rev. 21:24-26).

Still within the range of glory as something characteristic of human beings, we note that it can mean approval or praise or fame (I Thess. 2:20, Eph. 3:13, Rom. 11:12, Luke 14:10, I Cor. 4:10, I Cor. 12:26, I Thess. 2:6, Matt. 6:2). Sometimes the connotation is good (I Cor. 12:26) and other times evil, as with the hypocrites (Matt. 6:2).

One of the more interesting passages is Romans 9:4, which states that one of the great benefits of Israel was that it was given *the glory.* Most commentators take this to mean the shekinah glory of the tabernacle and then of the temple. Glory as a manifestation-form of the Lord is implied in Acts 7:2, where it is written that the God of glory appeared to Abraham. Gall[2] reports the contemporary belief that the manifestation to Abraham was a glorious manifestation.

---

1. Cf. *TWNT,* II, 250-251. Massie, "Glory (in N.T.)," *HDB,* II, 186. H. Kittel says that the connecting point with the interbiblical period is the eschatological-messianic aspects of glory. *Die Herrlichkeit Gottes,* p. 184.

2. *Die Herrlichkeit Gottes,* p. 92. Gall cites the parallels in the Targums.

The concept of the glory of God as a visible bright light is also found in the New Testament. Examples are the following: the shining of the glory of the Lord around the shepherds (Luke 2:9); the manifestation of glory at the transfiguration of Christ (Luke 9:21-23),[3] the shining of the bright light around Paul at the time of his conversion (Acts 9:22, 26); the filling of the heavenly temple with glory (Rev. 15:8); the shining of the glory of the Lord on the earth with the advent of the angel (Rev. 18:1); and the appearance of the glory of God in the New Jerusalem (Rev. 21:11).

SECTION 8: *The attribution of glory to God*

The highest point of worship in the New Testament occurs when the creature spontaneously and joyously glorifies God. This is not done abstractly or in a vacuum, but results from a recognition of God's gracious and mighty works. In Revelation 4 the four living creatures give God glory, honor, and thanks (v. 9), and whenever they do this the twenty-four elders give God glory, honor, and power because "thou didst create all things, and by thy will they existed and were created" (v. 11). Here it is the glory of God reflected in creation which calls forth adoration. Those in heaven who have conquered the beast fear and glorify God because "great and wonderful are thy deeds" (v. 3). Twice in Revelation 19 glory is sung to God by a great host: in the first instance because God has judged the great harlot (v. 2), and in the second instance because of the marriage of the Lamb (v. 7).

Two verses are especially interesting because they attribute glory directly to the nature of God. Peter calls God "the Majestic Glory" (II Pet. 1:17). Paul calls God "the Father of Glory" (Eph. 1:17), which implies many things, e.g., that he is a glorious God, that he gives glory, and that he is a being to whom glory belongs. Because of the close association with God and glory in the New Testament we find frequent doxological passages. In the midst of discussing the Church Paul breaks into doxological praise by saying: "To him be glory in the church and in Christ Jesus to all generations, for

3. The passage also mentions Moses and Elias appearing in glory. There is also the mention of cherubim of glory in Hebrews 9:5.

ever and ever. Amen" (Eph. 3:21). After a review of the history of God's purposes (Rom. 9-11) Paul writes: "For from him and through him and to him are all things. To him be glory forever. Amen" (Rom. 11:36). He ends the book of Romans and the final benediction with the words: "to the only wise God be glory forevermore through Jesus Christ!" (Rom. 16:27). Similar doxological passages are found in Galatians 1:5, I Timothy 1:17, Philippians 4:19, and Hebrews 13:21.

Because God is marked by glory, represented by glory, and surrounded by glory, glory is a sign of his nature. To know God properly is to know him in his glory. This is argued by Paul in Romans 1:21-23. Paul says that to turn from the true God to idolatry is *to turn away from the glory of God.* This is similar to Jeremiah 2:11. The only representation allowable of God is his glory and therefore idols are a sinful misrepresentation of the glory of God.

Romans 3:7 marks an interesting parallel to this. Paul says that his own falsehood nevertheless abounds to the glory of God. He has spoken of man's wickedness as showing the *justice* of God (v. 5) and in v. 7 changes it to the glory of God. The integrity of God is his justice and his justice is part of his perfection and therefore of his glory. To display the justice of God is therefore to magnify the glory of God.

SECTION 9: *The attribution of glory to things*

The New Testament not only ascribes glory to God but also to things. We have in Ephesians 1 the most sustained treatment in Scripture of salvation arising in the counsels of glory, gloriously manifested in Christ, and brought to individuals by the glorious gospel, who in turn hope for the glory that shall be revealed. Thus the entire gospel brings glory and rebounds to the glory of God (cf. vv. 6, 12, 14).

Paul attributes the resurrection of Christ to the glory of God (Rom. 6:4). We are reminded of the word of our Lord in John 11 in which he said that to see the resurrection of Lazarus is to see the glory of God (vv. 23, 40). The resurrection was a *manifestation* of the divine power and as such it revealed the glory of God. Hence Paul can speak of Christ being raised by the glory of God and therefore his resurrection is a glorious resurrection (cf. Phil. 3:21).

The gospel is closely connected with glory in its origin, in its blessings, and in its consummation. Paul calls it a glorious gospel (I Tim. 1:11) and that through the gospel we have Christ in us, the hope of glory (Col. 1:27). Furthermore, the preaching of the gospel partakes of the structure of glory. When the gospel wins its way, and is heard, and is believed, it has had a glorious course (II Thess. 3:1). When men receive the gospel, the name of Jesus Christ and God is glorified (II Thess. 1:12). Those who hear and believe feel called upon to give God the glory (Acts 13:48). The apostles who travel and preach the gospel do it for the glory of God (II Cor. 8:9). The Christians who have received the gospel are able to persevere in it according to the riches of glory which are theirs through the gospel (Eph. 1:16, Col. 1:11). Because Christians have shared in the gospel of the glory of God they are to receive each other to the glory of God (Rom. 15:7). Their faithfulness in trial redounds to the glory of Christ at his revelation (I Pet. 1:7, Jude 24). The greatest reward of God is to bestow glory, honor, and immortality (Rom. 2:7, 10), whereas one of the most severe of the final judgments is to be excluded from the glory of God (II Thess. 1:9).

Even more significant than these passages, however, is II Corinthians 3:7 to 4:6. Here we have a contrast between the glory of the law and the glory of the gospel. The law has a fading glory (3:7,11), but the gospel, which is the dispensation of the Spirit, brings a greater glory and a permanent glory. Its glory is so great that it makes the law appear as if it had no glory at all (v. 10). The splendor of the law was seen upon the face of Moses as a sort of afterglow, but the glory of the gospel shines fully in the face of Jesus Christ and that without fading (4:6).[4]

There are two passages of Scripture which use *doxa* in unusual ways (Rom. 3:23 and I Cor. 11:7). In the Romans passage man has sinned and come short of the glory of God. It is

---

4. This is admittedly a brief treatment, but the remainder of this book spells out the glory of the gospel in more detail, particularly in its eschatological realization.

customary for commentators to take the *doxa* of God here to mean either the divine perfection or the divine approval. It has been pointed out in recent literature,[5] however, that man was created sharing in the divine glory which he lost at the fall. Thus the passage means that man lacks his original created glory. *Doxa* in this passage does not, then, refer to God's perfection nor to his approval, but to the original status of man.

The Corinthians passage mentions that man is the image and glory of God, and that the woman is the glory (*doxa*) of man. Paul explains this in terms of the order of creation, namely, that the woman was created after the man. The meaning seems to be that just as man reflects the perfection of the work of God, woman reflects the perfection of the work of God as created from man.

5. *TWNT*, II, 249-250. "Saint Paul is no doubt alluding here to the rabbinic idea that Adam was created with a ray of the divine glory on his face, and that this was one of six things lost at the fall" A. M. Ramsay, *The Glory of God and the Transfiguration of Christ*, p. 46n.

III The Glory of Jesus Christ

Section 10: *The New Testament represents Jesus Christ as possessing a pre-incarnate glory.*

One of the most surprising features of the New Testament is the manner in which it occasionally associates Jesus Christ with the Yahweh of the Old Testament. This is seen in giving him the name of Lord (*Kurios*), in ascribing creation to him (Heb. 1:3) and the prerogative of judgment (John 5:27). It is also seen in the attribution to Jesus Christ of a divine glory. When we recall that according to the Old Testament the glory of the Lord is unique and incommunicable, the New Testament teaching about the glory of Christ becomes a most astounding doctrine. Not only does the New Testament make this attribution, but it does so with extraordinary fullness.[1] Wilhelm Thüsing has written two hundred and ninety-four pages on the glory of Christ in John's gospel alone.[2]

In two passages of the New Testament Jesus Christ is called the "Lord of glory" (I Cor. 2:8, Jas. 2:1). In I Corinthians 2:8 the princes of this world are accused of crucifying the Lord, who is characterized by glory.[3] The Revised Standard Version translates James 2:1 as follows: "My brethren, show no partiality as you hold the faith of our Lord Jesus Christ, the Lord of glory." There is a problem in rendering the Greek words *tou kurios hēmōn iēsou xristou tēs doxēs*, which the RSV solves by repeating the word "Lord" twice. The Züricher Bible similar-

---

1. Cf. *TWNT*, II, 251, 2, "Die Doxa Jesu."
2. *Die Erhöhung und Verherrlichung Jesu in Johannesevangelium.* This is a most thorough work with much attention given to lexical, exegetical, and theological elements.
3. The genitive of characterizing quality. *EGT*, II 779: "It signifies the entire grandeur of the incarnate Lord."

ly translates it as follows: "Jesus Christus, unsern Herrn der Herrlichkeit." Other scholars, however, take the expression as a genitive apposite and translate, "our Lord Jesus Christ, The Glory," i.e., the Shekinah.[4] Either way we have a clear and remarkable attribution of glory to Jesus Christ which is nothing short of breathtaking in view of the Old and New Testamental teaching concerning the glory of God.

Equally remarkable is the expression of Hebrews 1:3, "who being the radiance of his glory." The author sets forth the seven remarkable characteristics of the Son of God through whom the God of the prophets has spoken his final word of salvation. One of these marvelous characteristics of the Son is that he is the splendor of the divine glory. The notion is not of a beaming out of radiant glory but of a reproduction of that glory.[5] One could say that Christ's glory is a faithful reproduction of the original glory of God. Thus the Son is the Lord of Glory, and the Glory, and the reflection of the glory of God.

Most remarkable of all are the two assertions of the great seventeenth chapter of John wherein Christ speaks of having a glory before (pro) the creation of the world (vv., 5, 24).[6] "And now, Father, glorify thou me in thy own presence with the glory which I had with thee before the world was made. . . . Father, I desire that they also, whom thou hast given me, may be with me where I am, to behold my glory which thou hast given me in thy love for me before the foundation of the world."

These verses contain a number of features which can be touched upon only briefly. First, the pre-existence of Christ is an absolute presupposition if these verses are to make any sense. As Simon has so tellingly noted, this does not mean the pre-existence of heavenly beings in a heavenly hierarchy

4. So EGT, IV, 435. A. M. Ramsay sets forth both possibilities and settles for the genitive of apposition. Thus he translates it, "Our Lord Jesus Christ, the glory." The Glory of God and the Transfiguration of Christ, p. 149.

5. For a summary of opinions ancient and modern cf. C. Spicq, L'Épitre aux Hébreux, II, pp. 6-7. Citing Ménégoz, Spicq says the three things the verse states are the divine origin of the glory, its resemblance with God, and its personal independence (p. 7).

6. Cf. Thüsing, op. cit., pp. 205-221.

"but pre-existence prior to the world of space and time. . . .
Therefore the problem of the heavenly hierarchy does not
really exist, for the Son has not, as it were, the pre-eminence
among the cosmic powers but stands outside them, not in
merit but in essence."[7] Second, this glory is not the glory
manifested in the earthly life of Christ (John 1:14), nor the
glory given him in virtue of his passion (Phil. 2:9-11), but a
unique pre-temporal, pre-creation glory.[8] Both verses emphasize
this with the use of the preposition "before" (*pro*). Third,
this glory is not *separated* from the glory manifested in the
incarnation, nor in the coronation as the reward of our Lord's
suffering, but it is all part of the divine redemption, which
is a co-operative work of the Father and the Son. Fourth, we
observe the restoration of the pre-incarnate glory to the
Son, in the presence of the Father (*para seautō*), and grounded
in the eternal love of the Father for the Son. These are
remarkable Trinitarian and Christological passages. Finally,
the future beholding by the disciples of the glory of Christ
will be one of the greatest joys of redemption. The disciples,
too, are to be drawn into the relationship of love and glory that
characterizes the relationship of the Father with the Son.[9]

In view of such verses the Christology of the New Testament
could well be developed using the schema of glory with all its
aspects. So rich is this concept, and so truly is Christ associated
with the divine glory, that Paul's use of the expression "the
Lord of glory" is amply justified.

SECTION 11: *The New Testament presents Jesus Christ as
revealing the glory of God in his earthly life*

7. *Heaven in the Christian Tradition*, p. 96.
8. "This means the glory of Christ within the Godhead, his glory
as God." C. K. Barrett, *The Gospel According to St. John*, p. 429. "The
glory of the Eternal Word is distinguished from the glory of the Incarnate
Word . . . the spheres of life are different [i.e., the first is in the Godhead;
the second, on earth]." J. B. Bernard, *ICC, John*, II, 563.
9. Thüsing examines with some care the thought expressed so many
times of Christ's return to the Father which is the counterpart to the divine
sending by the Father. He notes John's use of such verbs as *metabainein,
hupagein, erxesthai, aperxesthai, aphienai*, and *anabainein. Op. cit.*, pp.
209ff.

in virtue of his being the Word-Incarnate and
the Sent-One of the Father

The most important passage in connection with the thesis
of this section is John 1:14, "And the Word became flesh
and dwelt among us, full of grace and truth; we have beheld
his glory, glory as of the only Son from the Father." We have
already indicated the pre-incarnate glory of Christ and affirmed
that it is of one piece with the incarnate glory of Christ.
Ramsay is correct, therefore, when he says that John 1:14
cannot be separated from John 1:1 any more than it can be
separated from the glory of the cross and the resurrection.[10]

The Word became flesh! The Word (looking backwards) is
the Word with God from all eternity, with God at creation,
and who is God himself.[11] The Word (looking forwards) is
Jesus of Nazareth, for *flesh* does not mean just body but the
entire person. The *became* of the text involves the full sweep
of events given to us in Philippians 2:5ff. It was a humiliation
and an impoverishment (II Cor. 8:9), including the historical
existence of Christ in Palestine as the son of Mary and citizen
of Nazareth. And in this flesh (*sarx*) he manifested his glory!

This glory was seen by the disciples. The verb employed
(*theasthai*) is, claims Bernard, never used of spiritual vision
but in twenty instances refers to physical seeing. Thus the
disciples beheld the glory of the Son in his earthly life and
not as a "supersensuous, mystical perception of spiritual
facts."[12] It was the perception of a glory peculiar to, and
fitting to, the only Son of the Father. It was a glory marked
with fullness, a fullness of grace and truth.

10. *Op. cit.,* p. 58.
11. *Kai theos en ho logos* — "And the Word was God" (John 1:1). These
words stand against all Arianism. Cf. Bruce Metzger, *The Jehovah's Witnesses
and Jesus Christ* (reprint from *Theology Today,* April, 1953). They also
stand firm against the Christology of religious liberalism or any modern
existential attempts to make Jesus only the symbol for God or the functional
existential equivalent of God. "*Theos* being without the article, is pre-
dicative and describes the nature of the word." Barrett, *op. cit.,* p. 130.
"We ought not to reinterpret this sentence in order to weaken its absolute-
ness and sharpness . . . . The evangelist means it literally when he calls
the Logos 'God.'" Cullmann, *Christology of the New Testament,* pp.
265, 267.
12. *Op. cit.,* I, 21.

The glory of the only Son manifested in the flesh is also the hidden content of many Old Testament passages. It is a messianic fulfillment. Isaiah saw this glory and spoke of it (John 12:41). There is a foregleam of this in the Targums, which affirm that in Isaiah 6 Isaiah saw "the glory of the *shekinah* of the King of the ages."[13] Here certainly the messianic-prophetic theme supplements the pre-existence-incarnation theme in the development of the glory of God in the Logos. At this juncture Thüsing is correct when he writes that "John 5:41 shows us then, that the line of the pre-existing *doxa* leads to the messianic revelation; the Son, who lives from eternity with the Father, is assuredly seen by the prophet as the One whose own person possesses the riches of the eternal glory but at the same time the One who will perform a work of revelation on the earth."[14]

Further amplification of the messianic-prophetic character of the glory of Christ is found in the Epistle to the Hebrews. In Hebrews 3:1 Christ is represented as our Moses and therefore the fulfillment of Moses and worthy of more glory than Moses (3:3). The author follows a similar line of argument concerning Aaron (5:5). Christ is our Aaron and therefore the fulfillment of Aaron, and he did not glorify (*edoxasen*) himself but was glorified of God to be a high priest.

The total life of the Son was both a manifesting of the glory of God and a glorifying of God in his complete dedication to the will and glory of the Father. Two Scripture passages give particular evidence for this. Luke 13 records the healing of the woman who had been bent over for eighteen years and the debate which followed between Christ and the ruler of the synagogue. Jesus refutes the ruler by arguing that a farmer shows more regard for an animal on the sabbath than the ruler does for a human being. Then Luke writes that "all the people rejoiced at the glorious things done by him" (v. 17).

The Greek expression for "glorious things" is *pasin tois endoxois*. Arndt and Gingrich's *Lexicon* render it "splendid

13. Barrett, *op. cit.*, p. 360. Bernard, *op. cit.*, II, 452.
14. *Op. cit.*, p. 219.

deeds." *It is an expression used of the extraordinary deeds
of the Lord in the Old Testament.*[15]

The second passage is John 2:11: "This, the first of his
signs, Jesus did at Cana in Galilee, and manifested his glory;
and his disciples believed in him." Here the miracle is a sign
which reveals the glory of Christ. Christ did this miracle
according to his own decision and will (*epoiēsen*) and in so
doing he revealed (*ephanerōsen*) his own (*autou*) glory. It
was thus the first miracle of a series of the same order.[16] In
other words, the subsequent miracles were of the same order
or character of this miracle *including the power to reveal the
glory of Christ.*

The glory of Christ in his earthly life, his *tenting* among
us (John 1:14), was a glory manifested in close connection with
God the Father. Our Lord constantly refused to recognize the
glory which comes from man, i.e., purely human approval
from human motives. "I do not receive glory from men," he
categorically said (John 5:41), and added that those who
sought for such a glory were spiritually wayward (cf. "How
can you believe, who receive glory from one another and do
not seek the glory that comes from the only God?" John 5:44).
The glory which comes from God is the glory bestowed in
salvation and in the name of Christ. It is, in Thüsing's expression, a Christological-soteriological glory.[17] The Son is absolutely free from this earthly, selfish, and sensuous self-
glorification, which in turn is so characteristic of unbelievers.

On the contrary, the complete selflessness of Jesus Christ,
and his complete devotion to the glory of his Father, is the
guarantee of his veracity, for "He who speaks on his own
authority seeks his own glory; but he who seeks the glory of
him who sent him is true, and in him there is no falsehood"
(John 7:18). This text is remarkable because it shows the

---

15. *TWNT*, II, 257.

16. Delling takes the first (*archē*) of this verse in this sense. *TWNT*,
I, 481. Barrett, however, says that "first" may "mean more than the
first of a series; not merely the first sign but 'a primary sign,' because
representative of the creative and transforming work of Jesus as a whole."
Op. cit., p. 161. The two interpretations do not necessarily exclude each
other.

17. *Op. cit.*, p. 201.

connection between truth and a true person. From the biblical perspective a person with a perfect devotion to God and his glory is incapable of speaking a lie (adikia) but is capable of speaking only the truth. Christ's perfect devotion to the glory of the Father and his complete renunciation of his own glory is the spiritual warranty for the complete veracity (alēthēs) of what he is. The Greek says, literally, he is true! In such a person there is no falsehood. Falsehood (adikia) is the antonym for truth or truthfulness.[18]

"If I glorify myself, my glory is nothing; it is my Father who glorifies me, of whom you say that he is your God" (John 8:54). Here we have the complete dependence of the Son upon the Father as well as the complete unity of the Father with the Son. *This verse conveys the spirit of the entire gospel of John.*[19] The glorious works of the Saviour are works of the Father glorifying the Son; and the Son has completely surrendered and devoted himself to the glory of the Father. Thus the words and deeds of Christ *are witnesses to the Father and of the Father.*[20]

Very similar to this verse is John 14:13, "Whatever you ask in my name, I will do it, that the Father may be glorified in the Son." The subject matter here is not the deeds and words of Christ but the answering of the disciples' petitions. The verse reflects the mutuality, however, of the Father and the Son. The Son answers prayers (note the strong, "I will do it," — poiēsō) out of motivation for the glory of God, but the Father in turn is glorified in and through the Son because the Son so acts.[21]

The counterpart to this glorious manifestation of Son and Father was the spontaneous glorification of God by the people of Palestine. "When the crowds saw it . . . they glorified

18. Cf. Barrett, *op. cit.*, p. 263. "In John 7:18 it is asserted that the truthfulness of Jesus, and with this the right of his claim in revelation, is grounded in the fact that he seeks the glory of the One who sent him." Thüsing, *op. cit.*, p. 199.

19. So Thüsing, *op. cit.*, p. 199.

20. Cf. Bernard, *op. cit.*, II, 319.

21. "The Father is glorified in the Son's activity, both in himself and through his followers, since in all things the Son seeks (and achieves) his Father's glory." Barrett, *op. cit.*, p. 384.

God" (Matt. 9:8); "and they glorified the God of Israel" (Matt. 15:31); "so that they were all amazed and glorified God" (Mark 2:12); "and he taught in their synagogues, being glorified by all" (Luke 4:15); "and . . . he . . . went home, glorifying God. And amazement seized them all; and they glorified God" (Luke 5:25-26); "fear seized them all; and they glorified God" (Luke 7:16); "she was made straight, and she [glorified] God" (Luke 13:13); "and all the people rejoiced at all the glorious things that were done by him" (Luke 13:17); "then one of them . . . turned back [glorifying] God with a loud voice" (Luke 17:15); "and immediately he received his sight and followed him, glorifying God" (Luke 18:43).

The raising of Lazarus plays a crucial role here. If the Cana miracle was the first sign by which the disciples saw his glory (and thus were prepared for other similar manifestations), the raising of Lazarus opens the concluding chapter of Christ's earthly life and so prepares the disciples for the crucifixion, resurrection, and ascension.

Upon hearing of the illness of Lazarus our Lord said that this was not unto a permanent death (for Lazarus did truly die) but a death "for the glory of God, so that the Son of God may be glorified by means of it" (John 11:4); and speaking to Martha he said, "Did I not tell you that if you would believe you would see the glory of God?" (v. 40).

Both Thüsing[22] and Ramsay[23] assert emphatically that the raising of Lazarus is of cardinal importance for our understanding of the redemptive work of Christ. This was not another sign-miracle among others, nor was it solely a personal favor, although Christ's personal love must not be undervalued. It was the beginning of the end; it was the commencement of the "hour" of divine appointment; it was the mirroring of his own decease and resurrection, showing before his own passion that he was the Resurrection and the Life; it was prophetic of the manner in which his passion and resurrection would glorify the Father.

22 *Op. cit.*, p. 229.
23 *Op. cit.*, p. 66.

SECTION 12:   *The New Testament represents the filial and Messianic glory of Jesus Christ in the transfiguration*[24]

Few events recorded in the New Testament offer such a wealth of topics for historical and biblical research as the transfiguration. Every aspect of it has an Old Testament, inter-biblical, or rabbinic association. It is not our intention to probe all of these ramifications, but to treat the transfiguration insofar as it reveals the glory of Christ;[25] for as Riesenfeld remarks,[26] its chief intention is to represent the glory of the Messiah.

In understanding the transfiguration, especially as it relates to the glory of Christ, the dramatic elements present must not be overlooked. It took place in a dramatic setting — a high mountain.[27] It took place at a dramatic time —

24 Matthew 16:27-17:8, Mark 8:38-9:8, Luke 9:26-36, John 12:27-28?, II Peter 1:16-18.

25 Besides the material in commentaries, dictionaries, encyclopedias and the individual word-studies in *TWNT* there are a number of monographs on the subject. Each of these contains a bibliography. Riesenfeld's is the longest, running to twenty-three pages. Cf. G. H. Boobyer, *St. Mark and the Transfiguration Story*. A. M. Ramsay, *The Glory of God and the Transfiguration of Jesus Christ*. Harald Riesenfeld, *Jésu Transfiguré*. Joseph Blintzler, *Die neutestamentlichen Berichte über die Verklärung Jesu*. Eugen Dabrowski, *La Transfiguration de Jésu*.

Boobyer is excellent in summarizing and criticizing the various theories. Ramsay is valuable in summarizing the latest researches in *doxa* and their relationship to the transfiguration. Riesenfeld is replete with references to comparative religions. Blintzler is valuable for a detailed exegetical account of three synoptic passages. Dabrowski gives the best sustained exegesis.

Thüsing (*op. cit.*) maintains the thesis that although John does not mention the transfiguration the entire gospel is a commentary upon it.

Although most recent studies treat the transfiguration as messianic and apocalyptic, there are variations. Riesenfeld treats it from the kingly-coronation motif. Hans-Peter Müller treats it as the synthesis in the church of the divergent-themes of the Son of Man and Messiah ("Die Verklärung Jesu," *Zeitschrift für die Neutestamentliche Wissenschaft*, 51:56-65, 1960). Alan Richardson stresses the transfiguration as that of Christ, the New Moses (*An Introduction to the Theology of the New Testament*, p. 181ff.).

26 *Op. cit.*, p. 246.

27 Peter calls it a holy mountain (II Pet. 1:18). Riesenfeld points out how many dramatic and important things in the life of Christ are associated with mountains. The O. T., too, has its reminders. Although there has

when our Lord was praying (Luke 9:29). It took place during a dramatic hour — at night.[28] Of the three elements, certainly the most unusual would be the occurrence at night, for the accompanying effects would be heightened.

Matthew and Mark do not use the word glory (*doxa*) as Luke does (9:31, 32), but as Kittel remarks, they do spell out graphically (*Ausmalung*) the glory of Christ.[29] The transfiguration contains these three aspects relevant to our study:

(i) *The glory of Christ is represented in the radiant transformation of his garments.* In this transformation (*metamorphoō*)[30] of Christ both face and garments became radiant.[31] We do not know what color these garments were. The best that can be ascertained is that the *simlah*, the outward cloak, was usually patterned in broad stripes of black alternating with white or brown.[32] Tissot, after residing in Palestine for some time to ascertain local colors, decided to paint the boy Jesus' cloak with dark red and white stripes.[33] Only the very wealthy were able to own a pure white wool garment; this was because the sheep whose wool was used for such garments had to be kept entirely free from dirt and manure stains.

Thus the transformation from a drab or a least a colored *simlah* to one of radiant white, with the night as a backdrop, was unusually striking. Mark says that his garments became whiter than any bleacher could make them. He uses an

---

been a sustained and ancient preference for Mt. Tabor, most recent writers prefer Mt. Hermon, which is over 9,000 feet high. Dabrowski argues strongly against Tabor. *Op. cit.*, pp. 52-53.

28 Cf. Plummer, *Luke, ICC.* p. 254. A. S. Martin, "Transfiguration," *Dictionary of Christ and the Gospels*, II, 743. Ramsay, *op. cit.*, p. 112.

29 Cf. *TWNT*, II, 252.

30 "This Greek word is the exact equivalent of the Latin-English words *transfigure* and *transform*." Gould, *Mark, ICC*, p. 161fn. Behm sees the transfiguration as apocalyptic imagery. Christ is the Son of Man of the End-Time. What the Messiah promises in the New World now is. *TWNT*, IV, 765.

31 Riesenfeld is correct in saying that the *doxa* is not a third something but characteristic of the transformation of the garments and the face. *Op. cit.*, p. 246.

32 Cf. M. S. and J. L. Miller, *Encyclopedia of Bible Life*, "What were the Garments of Jesus?" (pp. 60ff.).

33 *Ibid.*, p. 61. The Millers prefer dark red or blue. Douglas, they remark, chose brown in *The Robe*.

interesting word, *stilboō,* which is used in the Greek Bible only of the stars and precious metals. Here, along with the use of *phōs* (light) by Matthew, the similarity to stars must have first preference.

This radiant white is an eschatological color, particularly befitting heaven.[34] It is a super-worldly and super-earthly color which not only represents the glory that is above but also the glory that shall be.

(ii) *The glory of Christ is represented in the radiant transformation of the face of Christ.* Matthew says that his face shone as the sun. The verb *lampō* means to shine out, to shine forth, to glow. It is used by Paul in II Corinthians 4:6 to represent the creation light of the first day. The beaming face of Christ is a sign of his divine sonship and messianic glory as well as an anticipation of his future revelation.[35]

Luke's narration is different. He writes that the appearance (*eidos*) of his face became (*egeneto*) different (*heteros*). His face became other than what it was, i.e., it became glorious, for Luke uses *doxa* twice in the account. He writes that the three disciples saw him in his glory, the glory that was rightfully and uniquely his.

One cannot discuss the radiant face of Christ without a passing notice to II Corinthians 3 and 4. The glory of the Lord shining on the face of Moses causes Moses' face to become radiant. But this is a passing radiance, for only in Christ is the full radiance of the glory of God permanent and not transient. Christ as the image (*eikōn*) of God can bear in his face the full blaze of the glory of God, for he not only reflects the glory of God but also possesses within himself his own unique glory.

Many of the older opinions about the transfiguration represent it as an inward release of a restrained glory, but this is hardly the picture. The verb is passive — he was transformed. It is not so much a looking backward to John 1:1 and 1:14

34 *TWNT,* IV, 252.
35 *TWNT,* IV, 25. Lohse, *TWNT,* VI, 776, refers to Luke 9:29 as picturing an epiphany.

as it is a looking forward to the celestial glory of the Messiah.[36]

(iii) *The glory of Christ was manifested in the epiphany.* When Peter was confused and afraid from seeing Christ speaking with Moses and Elijah, he blurted out a request for the erection of shelters for the two men from heaven — had they already put up their own shelters for the night stay?[37] This was hardly uttered when a luminous cloud suddenly materialized (which was striking in the night time) and from the cloud came the words, "This is my beloved Son; listen to him" (Mark 9:7).

II Peter 1:16-18 lays stress on the epiphany as a giving of glory to Christ. Peter speaks of being an eyewitness (*epoptai*) of the majesty of Christ (*megaleiotēs*) which he equates with Christ's reception of honor (*timē*) and glory (*doxa*) from God the Father. Now, in an interesting turn of words, Peter calls the Father "The Majestic Glory." The majesty, the honor, the glory of Christ rests upon his divine sonship, for as Dabrowski comments, these words teach "the reality and transcendental divine sonship of Jesus Christ."[38]

---

36 So Riesenfeld, *op. cit.*, p. 247. Dabrowski comments: "St. Luke and St. Peter, in depicting the *doxa* of the Christ in the transfiguration, wish to say that the *form of God* in Christ with respect to its exterior manifestation had the same splendor which characterized the theophanies of the Old Testament, a splendor which the New Testament in following the example of the Septuagint has justly expressed by the term *doxa*." *Op. cit.*, p. 80.

37 Jeremias says that besides being figures of the End-Time, Moses and Elijah represent the suffering-pattern of the End-Time and this accounts for their speaking with Christ of his demise (*exodus*, Luke 9:31) at Jerusalem. *TWNT*, II, 941. Riesenfeld sees in Moses and Elijah the messianic-eschatological. *Op. cit.*, pp. 248-250.

What does *exodos* mean? (i) If a very close philological position is taken, the word simply means the death of Christ at Jerusalem. So Michaelis, *TWNT*, V, III. However, Michaelis says that the resurrection could be included in the word *exodos* only if Luke 9:22 could be brought opposite 9:31. (ii) Other scholars take *exodos* to mean the death, resurrection and ascension. First, the word itself suggests the recapitulation of the redemption out of Egypt so that death itself does not bear the weight of the significance wound up in the word. Second, *eisodos* is used of Christ's coming into this world (Acts 13:24), so *exodos* must mean Christ's departure. Cf. Plummer, *Luke, ICC*, p. 251. Ramsay, *op. cit.*, p. 123. Dabrowski, *op. cit.*, pp. 87-88.

38 *Op. cit.*, p. 102.

No doubt the transfiguration looks backward to the truth of
John 1:14, backward to the baptism of Jesus, backward to
Peter's confession.   Its immediate force was to reveal the
divine sonship of Christ and his messianic and celestial glory.
It looked forward to the cross, to remind the disciples that
when he was crucified he was crucified as the Lord of glory;
it looked forward to the coming kingdom and glory of Christ.
Peter represents the transfiguration as the dress-rehearsal of
the power and coming (*parousia*) of our Lord Jesus Christ.

Thus the transfiguration stands as a most unusual and powerful event in the unfolding of the life of the Son of God and
the course of divine redemption and in the history of the
divine glory.   It reminds us that the Glory took up its home in
a new temple, the body of Christ (cf. John 1:14, 2:19-22).
It looks forward to the day when the body crucified in humility and weakness will be raised by the glory of the Father
(Rom. 6:4), and it promises a day when the suffering servant
shall appear the second time, without sin and unto salvation,
as The Word of God who makes his glorious appearance upon
a white horse (Rev. 19:11-12).

SECTION 13:   *The New Testament represents the cross as the*
occasion for the glorification of Christ

In understanding the thesis of this section two more assertions
must be made.   First, the cross is not a revelation of glory as
the transfiguration was, but the *occasion* for glorification.   It
was not glorious in itself, but a bloody, painful, fearful, dis-
graceful mode of execution.   Second, although the cross is
the supreme and *the* unique event in the life of Christ, this
does not detract from the unity of revelation, redemption, or
the glory of Christ.   It is one mountain range with one
towering peak.

(i) In understanding the cross as the occasion of the
glorification of Christ it is indispensable to understand the
use of the Greek words hour (*hōra*) and time (*kairos*).[39]
The very first item which emerges from a study of these two

39 To keep the exposition clear we shall use the Greek words in the
following exposition.   *Hora* means "hour" and then, especially in John's
Gospel, a period of time whose origin is in the divine appointment.   *Kairos*

words is that the life of Christ was completely determined and defined by the will of the Father. Nobody could arrest Christ prior to his hour. His life moved on its course according to the *hora* and *chronos* and *kairos* of the Father. Secondly, as Thüsing observes, the "employment of the concepts of *hora* and *kairos* sets the entire earthly work of Jesus in relation to the event of his glorification (most of all his passion) ."[40] The death of Christ is at the same time a great troubling and distress of his soul and the occasion for his glorification. It is a fearful and terrible *hōra* to keep, but in it the Son is glorified.[41]

The *kairos* and the *hōra* can be traced in John's Gospel commencing with John 2:4. In this verse Christ makes it clear that it is *his* hour, *his* divine appointment. The critical moment is John 12:23, where our Lord says that the *hōra* has come. Thus begin the final hours, which do not end until the stilled body of the Lord of glory is rested in the new tomb. It moves from the supper room to Gethsemane to the trial to the *via dolorosa* to Calvary and then to the burial in the garden tomb. In this terrible *kairos* and through this dreadful *hōra* the Son of God is glorified. From there it moves to the second state, the *hōra* for the return to the Father, but a return through the cross (John 13:1) .

In John 12:23 our Lord says that the *hōra* has come. The divine appointment is now being kept; *chronos* (time) is now being filled with divine significance and thus is becoming *kairos*. In this hour the Son of Man[42] will be glorified (a

---

means time (*chronos*) filled with significance of meaning. Delling summarizes the latest lexical studies in *TWNT*, III, 456ff. *Kairos* in the New Testament has an intense theological-soteriological meaning. There is no English word which really translates it. Cf. Oscar Cullmann, *Christ and Time*, for the various Greek words and their significance.

40 *Op. cit.*, p. 99. We are deeply indebted to Thüsing for much of this section. No other writer has so exhaustively and carefully treated these themes in John's gospel.

41 The paradox is very clear in John 12:27-28 with the troubling of the soul of Christ (v. 27) , and yet the prayer for the glorification of the Father (v. 28) .

42 For the recent research on this subject (Son of Man) and its meaning in John's Gospel, cf. Cullmann, *Christology of the New Testament*, Chapter 6; and Thüsing, *op. cit.*, pp. 258ff. With John it is an intense Christological, incarnational, and messianic title.

passive verb). But even though this is the occasion for the glorification of the Son it is not a glorious experience. It is true that the impelling motive is joy (Heb. 12:2), nevertheless with the coming of the *hōra* comes the troubling of the soul (*tarassō*, to be troubled, to be disturbed, John 12:27). With the intensity of the disturbance — loud cries, tears (Heb. 5:7), bloody sweat — comes the idea of evading such a frightening *hōra* — "and what shall I say? save me out of this hour?" But this is rejected because "for this cause (*dia touto*) I came unto this *hōra*." No evasion is possible because the greatest meaning, the deepest significance, and the highest import of the incarnation is to be found in this *hōra*." For this reason (*dia touto*) Christ became poor (II Cor. 8:9), emptied himself (Phil. 2:6), and took on flesh (John 1:14). The entire life of Christ heads in the direction of this *dia touto* and finds its final rationale at this point.

The possibility of evasion is rebuffed with a second great assertion: "Father, glorify thy name!" The *hōra* must be kept. If this *hōra* is not kept then the great weight of the incarnation is trivialized. But this *hōra* must be kept to the glory of God. The obedience to the demand of the hour must be such that the name and character of God will be glorified in the *hōra*. This great petition is answered with a voice from heaven: "I have glorified it, and I will glorify it."

The language here is very strong. The *hōra* of Christ is the will of God, the supreme will of God, the unavoidable will of God. It was a divine imperative of the highest order. This *hōra* is the summit of the life of Christ, the maximum work of Christ, and the most important accomplishment of Christ. Every purely incarnational theology fails when it deals exegetically with John's teaching that the cross is the unique *hōra* of Christ. An incarnational theology maintains that Bethlehem is as important as Calvary; that a redemptive life simply comes to a redemptive climax. But it fails to see the uniqueness of the event of the cross itself as the *hōra* of the Father determined for the Son and accepted by the Son in filial obedience. Any future attempts to defend an incarnational theology must come to grips with Thüsing's book.

John 7:6 is very decisive where our Lord says to his brothers that their time is *always* here. Our Lord's *kairos* was fixed by the will of the Father and therefore did not come into existence until the time arrived which was set by the Father. It came into reality at the time fixed by John 12:23. Purely human opportunities are, in contrast, generally available. If the incarnation were the redemptive deed itself, our Lord could never have uttered these words, for his *hōra* and *kairos* would have been ready (*etoimos*) during his entire incarnate life. But John's teaching is that this is not so. The incarnation looks forward to the cross as its *raison d'être,* and the cross looks back on the incarnation as its presupposition.

(ii) The New Testament represents the cross as the event in which the Father glorifies the Son, and in which the Son glorifies the Father by always obeying the will of the Father, so fulfilling and completing the work of the Father.[43] The notion of the work and works of Christ is in itself an important study in John's gospel. The entire life of Christ is doing the work and works of God to the glory of God. In Staufer's words, "the life of Christ is an acted doxology."[44] Our Lord says that his food is to do the will of the Father who sent him and to accomplish his work (John 4:34); that his works are the works of God manifest in him (John 9:3); that the works he does prove his special unity and union with the Father (John 10:38); that the Father within him does his works (John 14:10); and that at the end of his life he has completed and fulfilled the work of the Father (John 17:4).

Thus the work of the Father and the Son are one; the Son glorifies the Father in his complete obedience to the Father; the Father glorifies the Son in virtue of his obedience. This same pattern pertains to the cross, for the cross is the final, climactic work of Jesus Christ. Only in the cross do we have the "for this reason" — *dia touto.*

The cross is the greatest *ergon* (work) of God and of the Son. Therefore when the *hōra* and the *kairos* of the cross come, the Son prays: "Glorify thy Son that the Son may glorify thee" (John 17:1). Thüsing has put it this way:

43 The biblical word "work" (*ergon*) is a very important one, one which the English word does not do justice to. Cf. *ergon, TWNT,* 631ff. The material relevant to John's Gospel is found on page 639.

44 *New Testament Theology,* p. 28.

If we compare the content of the *hōra* with the "completion of the work," we see readily that both are closely bound together. The hour of glorification (of Jesus himself) is the hour of the completion of the work (through which the Father is glorified), and the event, which is elevated as the first in line as the content of the hour and as the completion of the work, is the passion, particularly, the death of Jesus, and to be sure as the accomplishment of obedience.[45]

Bultmann believes that the conception of the cross as a glorification is opposed to the concept of the cross as an atonement.[46] But this would be the case only if the cross were a glorification in and of itself. However, glorification does not pertain to the cross *per se* but is the reward of the cross. In doing the work of reconciliation the Son glorifies the Father, for what else could glorify God more than effecting the redemption of the world? In being the Reconciler, Christ does glorify the Father.

This is consonant with two other passages of Scripture. Paul speaks of glorying in the cross (*kauxaomai*, Gal. 6:14). The bearing of our curse (Gal. 3:13) was certainly the essence of vicarious atonement and calls forth from Paul a boasting. The cross, to Paul, stands in amazing contrast to Jewish schemes. The other passage is Revelation 5, in which the Lamb of God who was slain to redeem (*agoradzō*) us to God is given power, wealth, wisdom, might, honor, and glory. The work of the Lamb in redemption is the occasion for attributing glory to him.

SECTION 14: *The New Testament represents the resurrection of Christ as a glorification of Christ.*

The hour of Christ, which came to its climax upon the cross, looked backward to its divine appointment and to the *hour* of leaving this world and going to the Father (John 13:1). The glorification of the cross is followed by the glorification of the resurrection. The latter has two noteworthy aspects:

(i) Christ's body was changed into a glorious body. Paul

45 *Op. cit.,* p. 100.
46 *Theology of the New Testament,* II, 52ff.

mentions that Christians shall have bodies which shall be conformed to the glorious body of Christ (Phil. 3:21). The body of Christ in his earthly life was like our bodies (Rom. 8:3), but at the resurrection it underwent a change and became a glorious body. The apostle, in I Corinthians 15:42ff., spells out the kind of spiritual body the redeemed shall have. All the positive characteristics of man's new body are also true of Christ's risen body — namely, imperishability, glory, power, and spirituality.

In Romans 6:4 Paul writes that Christ was raised from the dead by the glory of the Father, and uses this transformation of body to explain the spiritual transformation of the Christian. This transformation is represented as a *resurrection* by the glory of the Father. Here is one of the passages in which glory shades over into power or might.[47] The risen body of our Lord is a reflection of the glory of God and a bearer of that glory.

(ii) The resurrection of Christ was into a state of glory. His body not only underwent a change into a glorious body but his Person entered a glorious state. Our Lord told his disciples that the Messiah must suffer and then enter into his glory (Luke 24:26). Peter mentions the puzzlings of the prophets over the sufferings of Christ and his subsequent glory (I Pet. 1:11). Paul states that by the resurrection from the dead God set forth Christ powerfully, or in power, as the Son of God (Rom. 1:4). There is some debate over the meaning of the word "declared," (*horizō*).[48] Schmidt makes the point that in this passage we do not have, so to speak, Christ *made* the Son of God, for that would overlook the New Testament teaching of the pre-existence of Christ. The resurrection *declares* or *designates* Jesus Christ in a manner which cannot be equivocated. In virtue of this divine *designating* Christ enters into a state of glory, of power, of Lordship.[49]

Thus the risen Christ is in a state of majesty (*megaleiotēs,*

---

47 Cf. Ramsay, *op. cit.,* p. 31. "It is power viewed externally rather than internally; the stress is laid not so much in the inward energy as on the signal and glorious manifestation." Sanday and Headlam, *op. cit.,* p. 157.

48 Sanday and Headlam, *op. cit.,* p. 7. Schmidt, *TWNT,* V, 454.

49 This is how Cullmann takes the expression, *op. cit.,* p. 292.

II Pet. 1:16), of universal authority (*exousia*, Matt. 28:18),
and of glory (I Pet. 1:21 — "God raised him from the dead
and gave him glory"). Parallel to the word of Peter in his
letter are his words in Acts 3:13, "The God of Abraham and
of Isaac and of Jacob, the God of our fathers, glorified his
servant Jesus, whom you delivered up and denied in the presence
of Pilate, when he had decided to release him." This passage is
important not only because it reveals the action of Christ in
the early Church and clearly witnesses to the resurrection-
faith of that early church ("whom God raised from the dead,"
v. 15) but it speaks of Jesus Christ as the servant of the God
of the fathers. God has glorified his servant (*ebed Yahweh*,
pais theou),[50] the Author of life (v. 15). Here is a concept
and a speech which go deeply into the Old Testament. The
death of Christ was foretold by the prophets (v. 18); he was
the subject of a prophetic utterance by Moses (v. 22); and
witnessed to by all the prophets from Samuel afterwards (v.
24). The suffering servant of the prophets is identified with
Jesus, and this Cullmann calls the most primitive Christology
of the church.[51] But the suffering servant has now, by the
resurrection, become the glorified Lord.

SECTION 15: *The New Testament represents the glory of
Christ in his ascension*

The ascension is described by Paul in I Timothy 3:16 as a
taking up into glory. This clearly places the ascension within
the structure of the glorification of Christ. There is much
indirect evidence for the ascension, as is pointed out by J. G.
Davies in *He Ascended into Heaven;* in addition, there is a

---

50 This concept of the suffering servant has been the subject of much
research in recent years. Cf. Zimmerli and Jeremias, *TWNT*, V, 653-712.
Cullmann, *op. cit.*, pp. 73f. 78f. J. E. Ménard, "Pais Theou as Messianic
Title in the Book of Acts," *The Catholic Biblical Quarterly*, 19:83-92, Jan.,
1957. H. H. Rowley, *The Servant of the Lord and Other Essays on the
Old Testament*. C. R. North, *The Suffering Servant in Deutero-Isaiah*.
    51 *Op. cit.*, p. 73. Cullmann calls it an *ebed Yahweh* Christology.
Zimmerli and Jeremias' *TWNT* article is translated as *The Servant of
God* in the series, *Studies in Biblical Theology*, No. 20. In this they write:
"The result is that there is no area of the primitive Christian life of faith
which was not stamped by *ebed* Christology" (p. 98).

direct account.[52] The event as such is recorded three times in the New Testament, although two of the passages are textually suspect. Mark 16:19 reads, "So then the Lord Jesus, after he had spoken to them, was taken up into heaven, and sat down at the right hand of God." Luke 24:50-51 reads, "Then he led them out as far as Bethany, and lifting up his hands he blessed them. While he blessed them, he parted from them." Some manuscripts add "and was carried up into heaven." Davies believes that the latter words are part of the original text because an excision is easier to explain than an insertion.[53] Even so, however, the ascension may well be implied by the correlation of "he parted from them," i.e., into heaven, and the fact that "they returned to Jerusalem with great joy." The one secure passage is the account in Acts 1:1-11, though the ascension is expressed in many other passages of the New Testament and implied by still others.[54]

The ascension is not to be reduced to a phase of the resurrection. It is, as Ramsay points out, the counterpart to the downward or coming movement of the incarnation.[55] Or as Staufer says it: "In the ascension Jesus attained to the highest point of his *anabasis,* the provisional end of his journey."[56] The cloud, according to Richardson, is a traditional symbol

52 Davies writes: "The witness of the New Testament writings to the Ascension of Christ is remarkable in its universality. We have observed references to it in all four Gospels, in the Acts of the Apostles, in the Pauline Epistles, in the Epistle to the Ephesians and to the Hebrews, in the Pastorals, in I Peter and in the Book of Revelation. We may confidently assert therefore that the inclusion of the words 'he ascended into heaven' in the Apostles' Creed is amply justified by the evidence." Pp. 45-46.

53 *Ibid.,* p. 41.

54 Bultmann considers the ascension as legendary (*The Theology of the New Testament,* I, 45) and as a gnostic myth (I, 176, 177). Major feels that modern astronomical theory rules out a physical assumption of the body of Christ, so the ascension means Jesus' entrance into "the eternal invisible sphere," *The Mission and Message of Jesus,* I, 296. It could well be that "theological space" and astronomical space represent an instance of two inco-ordinables and not a contradiction. If so, Major's point is meaningless.

55 *Op. cit.,* p. 184.

56 *Op. cit.,* p. 138.

of the presence of God "into which the Lord has been received to share forever the power, the glory and the reign of God."[57]

(i) The ascension was an ascension into glory (". . . and was taken up into glory," I Tim. 3:16). Two passages in John's Gospel make it clear that the resurrection and the ascension constituted a glorification of Christ. In John 7:39 the coming of the Spirit is predicated upon the glorification of Christ. Ascending to the Father, the Son receives the gift of the Spirit which he then bestows upon the Church. This ascension is thus his glorification. With reference to the triumphal entry (John 12:16), the disciples did not understand the importance of it until Christ was glorified, i.e., ascended to the Father. Thus the ascension was both an ascension to glory and a glorification of the Son.

The ascension is richly represented in John's Gospel as a going back to the Father. Although the principal verb employed is *anabainō* — "to mount up, to go up, to ascend"[58] — a number of verbs are employed to indicate this important event.[59] This ascending (*anabainein*) is the counterpart to the descending (*katabainein*), i.e., the incarnation. But, as Thüsing notes, the return is a return through the cross.[60] The descent was through the incarnation and virgin birth; the ascent is a return to this glory.[61] To be exalted, to return to the Father, and to be glorified belong to the same continuum of events.

Two of the three most important passages concerning the ascension of Christ are John 3:13, where we read that the

---

57 *Op. cit.,* p. 200.

58 *Anabainō* is a word rich in religious and cultic significance. Cf. *TWNT,* I, 516-521. It is used for entering a temple, and for going up to Jerusalem. In the religious sphere it means to mount up to heaven. Peter connects the ascension of Christ with the session of Christ at the right hand of God. Acts 2:34, Ps. 110:1.

59 Thüsing lists them as *metabainein* (John 13:1); *hupagein* (John 7: 33, 8:14, 21f., 13:3, 33, 36, 14:4f., 28, 16:5, 10, 17; *poreuesthai,* John 14:2f., 12, 28, 16:7, 28; *erxesthai,* John 17:11, 13; *aperxesthai,* John 16:7; *aphienai,* John 16:28; and *anabainein,* John 3:13, 6:62, 20:17. *Op. cit.,* p. 209.

60 *Ibid.,* p. 259.

61 Thüsing points out that *anabainein, hupsōthēnai,* and *doxasthēnai* are parallel concepts and correspond to *katabainein. Ibid.,* p. 259.

Son of Man who descended shall ascend to heaven, and John 6:62, where Christ says to his disciples that they shall see the Son of man ascending to where he was before. In this rather long chapter the descent of Christ is described as being sent from the Father (vv. 29, 57), as the bread which comes down from heaven (vv. 33, 41-42, 51, 58), and   coming down from heaven to do the Father's will (v. 38). It is out of a sustained and theologically profound discussion of his descent into this world that Christ makes this profound remark concerning his return to heaven. Finally, in the third passage, Christ assures his disciples that he is ascending to "my Father and your Father, to my God and your God" (John 20:17).

The ascension is also called a taking up (analēpsis, analambanō). As already indicated, this is referred to in two textually suspect passages (Mark 16:19 and Luke 24:51). But it also occurs in Acts 1:2, 11, 22 and in I Timothy 3:19. Whereas Luke lays emphasis upon the actual events surrounding the ascension, Paul emphasizes the entrance of Christ into his divine majesty.[62]

(ii) The ascension represents the glory of Christ as his session at the right hand of God, the right hand being the place of honor.[63]   God did his great deeds with his right hand. At the last judgment the sheep go to the right side. The right side is the place of honor. The right side is the direction we metaphorically turn to in prayer. The right side is also the place of favor and exaltation. To be exalted to the right side of God is to be at the place of greatest honor, to receive the highest exaltation, and to be at the place of supreme glory. Therefore Christ's session at the right hand of God is an elevation to the highest pinnacle of glory.

This exaltation is expressed diversely in the New Testament. It is an exaltation to the right hand of God (Acts 2:33, 5:31); it is being raised from the dead to the right hand of God (Rom. 8:34); it is being above, seated at the right hand of God (Col. 3:1); it is being raised from the dead and made to sit at God's right hand in heavenly places (Eph. 1:20); it is a session at the right hand of the majesty on high (Heb. 1:3);

62 *TWNT*, IV, 8-9.
63 *"Deksios," TWNT*, II, 37f.

it is sitting at God's right hand until he makes the Son's enemies his footstool (Heb. 1:13); it is being seated at the right hand of the throne of majesty in heaven as a high priest (Heb. 8:1); it is a session at the right hand of God after having offered a perfect sacrifice (Heb. 10:12); it is a session at the conclusion of the earthly race (Heb. 12:2); it is a going into heaven to be at the right hand of God after the resurrection and there becoming Lord of principalities and powers; and it is receiving the Name that is above every name (Phil. 2:6-11).

It is this Christ whom Stephen saw when dying (Acts 7:55); whom Paul met on the Damascus Road (Acts 9:3-6); upon whose face believers see the radiant glory of God (II Cor. 4:4); whom John encountered at the isle of Patmos (Rev. 1:12-16); whom the writer of Hebrews sees as the last Adam crowned with honor and glory (Heb. 2:7-9).

(iii) Following his session Christ is glorified in his intercession, in the work of the Spirit on earth, and in the ministry of his followers.[64] As a great high priest he has passed through the heavens to the right hand of God. There Stephen saw him in glory ready to intercede for him and to receive him at death (Acts 7:55, Heb. 7:23-28, 9:24, 8:1). Further, our Lord told his disciples that they glorify the Father when they bear much fruit (cf. John 15:8, 17:10, 22). Finally, the Spirit will glorify the Son as he performs his work within believers (John 16:14).

SECTION 16: *The New Testament represents Christ's glory as a triumphal return at his second coming*

In close harmony with the eschatological framework of the New Testament is the structure of the two appearances of Christ. The first is the appearance in humility for the sacrifice of the cross, and the second is a manifestation in glory. These two appearings are clearly set forth in Hebrews 9:23-28. Cullmann says that Hebrews 9:28 settles it for certain that the New Testament does teach a literal return of Christ.[65] The

---

64 Cf. Thüsing, *op. cit.*, p. 107f., 141f.

65 *The Christology of the New Testament*, p. 103. Note the *ek deuterou*. This is against those who interpret *parousia* as being present with Christ and excluding a return of Christ.

very structure of New Testament Christology is suffering followed by glory — public suffering followed by public glory. John's witness is: "Behold, he is coming with the clouds, and every eye will see him, every one who pierced him; and all tribes of the earth will wail on account of him. Even so. Amen" (Rev. 1:7).

In the Gospels Jesus Christ is pictured as the Son of Man returning in power and glory to the world of his rejection, humiliation, and crucifixion. Three things are important in these references (Matt. 16:27, 19:28, 25:31, 24:30, Luke 22:69, 21:27, 9:6, Mark 8:38, 13:26). (i) The first is the very title, Son of Man. In these passages the Son of Man appears as the eschatological Saviour and Judge.[66] There is emphasis upon the judgment and the division which the Son of Man shall effect. As the Son of Man, Christ is the Lord of the Kingdom of God and its Judge. Taylor is correct when he expresses his opinion that "too little consideration has been given to the eschatological implications of Christ's lordship . . . the suggestion of a true superhuman dignity essentially belongs to the idea of the Son of Man as an eschatological figure, and when the genuineness of the sayings in which it is expressed is accepted, a divine consciousness to this extent must be attributed to Jesus."[67]

(ii) Second, we note the situation in which these remarks are made. Our Lord is on trial before his own people. He is the Son of Man, the Messiah, the Servant of the Lord and the Son of God. Yet, as Paul puts it, "he was crucified in weakness" (II Cor. 13:4). His claims were rejected and considered blasphemous. He was delivered over to the Roman authority and the death penalty requested. In this situation he reminds his crucifiers that he is the Son of Man and that he will make a second appearance on earth totally different from his first appearance. He will appear in the full dignity, power and glory of the Son of Man. Therefore they were not putting to death an ordinary person, but in Paul's language they were crucifying the Lord of glory.[68]

66 Bultmann, *Theology of the New Testament*, I, 79.
67 *The Person of Christ*, p. 158f.
68 As the scholars point out, the unique contribution of Jesus Christ to the concept of the Son of Man is that he linked it with suffering. Thus

(iii) Christ promises that the Son of Man will come in power and glory, in contrast to his apparent weakness and humility. The representations here are varied — the glory of the Father, the glorious throne, the right hand of power, power and great glory, his glory, glory of the Father, clouds and angels. Their impression is one and the same, namely, that the Son of Man shall return to this earth in an overwhelming display of power and glory. In Paul's letter the return of Christ is associated with the perfection or completion of salvation and this in turn is a manifestation of the glory of Christ (Titus 2:13, II Thess. 1:10). In the Epistle to the Hebrews the high priest of our profession is leading many sons to glory (Heb. 2:10) but he will return and perfect his work in us (Heb. 9:28). In Peter the glory of Christ at this return will balance off the sufferings of Christ in his first appearance (I Pet. 1:7, 5:1, 4, 10).

SECTION 17:   *The New Testament represents Jesus Christ as possessing an eternal glory in the ages to come*

That Christ shall have an eternal glory is implied by John 17:5, 24 where Christ asks to be glorified again with the glory he once possessed in eternity with the Father before creation. This is in keeping with other parts of the New Testament which ascribe an eternal glory to Jesus Christ (II Tim. 4:18, II Pet. 3:18, I Pet. 4:11, Rev. 5:9, 13).[69] Furthermore, this is a glory associated with and paralleling the glory of God the Father (Rev. 1:5-6, 21:23). Whitham has well stated this eternal glory of Christ:

> In the resurrection life, therefore, Christ will be seen and known by all the faculties, the whole being of man redeemed, as sharing fully and essentially the 'glory' of the Godhead. His

---

we have the typical New Testament pattern of his appearance for suffering and his appearance in glory.   Cf. Ramsay, *op. cit.*, p. 30; Bultmann, *op. cit.*, I, 31.

69 It must be said in passing that the Christology of religious liberalism could never make peace with the doctrine of the glory of Jesus Christ. Only a doctrine of the incarnation of God the Son in the human person of Jesus of Nazareth can bear the weight of the New Testament teaching of the glory of the Son.

was ever inseparable from it; His humanity will be seen filled full, illuminated by its union with His Divinity, 'taken up into God' . . . and so constituting the perfect expression and vehicle of His Divinity (John 3:2). Hence in the ideal and perfected Church, as described in the Apocalypse, both humanity and its material setting are illuminated with 'the glory of the Lamb,' whose glorified humanity is, as it were, the 'Lamp,' (Rev. 21:23) in which shines the 'glory' of the Godhead.[70]

70 "Glory," *Dictionary of Christ and the Gospels*, I, 649.

IV   The Foundations of Glorification

SECTION 18:   *General affirmations of glorification*

When Paul sets forth the great structure of divine redemption, glorification is listed as the final and concluding act of redemption (Rom. 8:30). Glorification is part of the total redeeming action of God and presupposes the foundations laid in the prior acts of redemption. Glorification has its foundation in the work of Christ as this is applied to believers.

(i) We have already noted that according to the Old Testament prophets (Ezekiel, Isaiah) there will be an eschatological manifestation of the glory of God. There are some verses in the Psalms, however, which speak of glory as something bestowed or given *to men*. In describing the great worth of serving the Lord and his great goodness to man, the Psalmist says that God gives favor and glory (84:11). Glory is used here in the sense of honor. In other passages glory seems to be the vindication of the righteous man, e.g., Psalm 62:7, "on God rests my deliverance and honor [*kabod*]," and in Psalm 3:3, "But thou, O Lord, art a shield about me, my glory, and the lifter up of my head." With reference to Psalm 3:3 Kraus notes that oppression and derision take a man's glory away but God restores it.[1]

The concept of final eschatological vindication as a bestowal of glory occurs most clearly, however, in Psalm 73:24: "Thou dost guide me with thy counsel, and afterward thou wilt receive me to glory." The theme of the Psalm is that the prosperity of the wicked greatly distresses the Psalmist. He gains no change of perspective on this problem until he goes into

---

1 *Psalmen*, I, 26 (*Biblischer Kommentar Altes Testament*).

the sanctuary. *Then* he realizes that during the course of this life he enjoys the guidance of the hand of the Lord, and afterwards he will receive his vindication, his glory (*kabod*). The wicked will be swept away in a judgmental flood but with glory shall the righteous be rewarded. This is an eschatological vindication, for as Kraus asserts, "Here can man speak with full right of an eschatological act of God, for all the limits of the Old Testament order of faith and life have been leaped over."[2]

In such verses we have only a suggestion, but withal a real suggestion, that in some future day God shall reward the righteous man with a final, complete, and perfect vindication, which is described as a bestowal of honor or *kabod*.

(ii) That God shall glorify his people is a clear New Testament teaching. The believer's glorification follows the pattern set by our Lord, namely suffering followed by glory. I Peter affirms the closest parallel between Christ and the Christian. The suffering of the Christian will be followed by subsequent glory (I Pet. 5:1, 4). Paul speaks a similar note in Romans 8:18 when he contrasts the present sufferings with the glory that shall follow, and in II Corinthians 4:17 he contrasts our present affliction with the eternal weight of glory which shall be ours.

This New Testament teaching is expressed not only in terms of suffering and glory, however, for three other pairs of contrasts can be found there. We are justified now and glorified then (Rom. 8:30).[3] Certainly in the analogy of Scripture this must mean future glorification. Romans 5:2 makes the contrast

2 *Ibid.*, I, 510. Kraus defends the vindication interpretation of glory in this verse in contrast to those who take glory to mean immortality or a reception into heaven.

3 The aorist, "he glorified," has puzzled commentators. Liddon takes it to mean that all the acts of redemption are contemplated as accomplished in the divine mind (*The Epistle to the Romans*, p. 140). Denney takes it to be the inseparable unity of the acts of salvation and not to be dissolved away with the trite assertion that to God all things are present. *EGT*, II, 652. Sanday and Headlam take the aorist to show the certainty of the divine accomplishment of our salvation, *Romans, ICC*, p. 218. H. Kittel says that *doxa* refers to our justification in its present and future states. *Die Herrlichkeit Gottes*, p. 197. Concerning Romans 8:30 he says that it shows that *doxa* is the necessary consequence of justification. He takes the aorist to mean the certainty of the divine act.

between present grace and future glory, i.e., between this present state of grace and the one it shall merge into. Colossians 3:1-4 sets forth the contrast between the present hidden life in Christ and its future manifestation in glory.

(iii) Just as the completed creation is called good, completed redemption is called glory. It is not only a being glorified (Rom. 8:30) but a sharing in Christ's glory (John 17:22), a wisdom of God decreed for our glorification (I Cor. 2:7), a preparation of vessels for glory (Rom. 9:23), a being called to eternal glory (I Pet. 5:10, II Pet. 1:3), a bringing of many sons to glory (Heb. 2:10), an eternal glory which goes with salvation (II Tim. 2:10), and an obtaining of the glory of Christ (II Thess. 2:14, I Thess. 2:12). That is to say, God has purposed to complete and end his salvation with glory. The finished work of creation was good but the completed work of redemption shall be glorious!

(iv) Although the completion of redemption is called glorification, it is also called a number of other things. Since it can be viewed as the continuance and full realization of salvation, glorification is itself called *salvation* (Heb. 9:28, I Pet. 1:5, Rom. 13:11). Insofar as it is the full working out of our salvation it is called a *perfecting* (Heb. 11:40, 12:23). Hebrews 12:2 calls Christ the Perfecter of our faith (cf. also Phil. 1:6).[4] Because God has purposed to bless us in Christ, the fullness of this blessing is our glorification. God has purposed to give us all things (Rom. 8:32), to make all things of the future peculiarly ours (I Cor. 3:22); to show to us in the ages to come our riches in Christ (Eph. 2:7); to restore all things (Acts 3:21) and to sum all things up in Christ (Eph. 1:10).

SECTION 19:   *The foundation of glorification in the work of Christ*

Christ is the foundation of our redemption. This is a clear New Testament teaching (I Cor. 3:11, Eph. 2:20, I Pet. 2:4-8). He is a foundation (*themelios*), a cornerstone (*akrogōniaios*), a stone (*lithos*), and a living stone (*lithos zōnta*). As the foun-

4 Cf. P. J. Du Plessis, *Teleios, The Idea of Perfection in the New Testament.*

dation of redemption he is therefore the foundation of our glorification.

(i) By his death he establishes the proper resolution of the question of our sins. However theologians may have differed over the nature of the atoning death of Christ, they agree that it was atoning, i.e., it did achieve the benefit for which it was designed. The death of Christ is the absolute foundation of redemption for in it sin received its divine counter-measure.

The New Testament represents the death of Christ as completely, thoroughly, and finally settling the matter of sin, sin in the three-fold sense of guilt, power, and defilement. The death of Christ establishes the righteousness of God (Rom. 3:25); it effects reconciliation (II Cor. 5:18-21);[5] it accomplishes a purification of sins (Heb. 1:3); it achieves a redemption (Eph. 1:7). There is a richness in the New Testament both regarding the manner in which the death of Christ is represented, and the benefits which it makes possible. The New Testament wishes to affirm clearly that *the death of Christ is a complete and satisfactory resolution of the problems created by our sins.* No matter which objective theory of the atonement we adopt, we must say at least this much.[6] And granted this fact, we believe that the analogy which does the most justice to the New Testament doctrine of the atonement is the *juridical* analogy. In its broadest sense this was the view of Anselm and the Reformers, and it received a classic statement in James

5 Certainly II Cor. 5:21 (Christ made sin for us) is a commentary on the death of Christ *before* the righteousness of God; i.e., the reconciliation effected by the atonement is based upon the atonement first satisfying the righteousness of God.

6 No subjective view of the atonement (namely, that the purpose of the atonement is to stimulate or arouse or ignite our religious life or powers or faith) can stand before the massive New Testament evidence that Christ died for our sins before God. (Not that there is *no* truth to the subjective interpretation of the atonement, for this much is affirmed in Heb. 2:2 and I Pet. 2:21).

Also to be resisted are recent existentialist theories which teach that atonement is not complete until there is the decision of faith. This is either carelessness in failing to keep separate the death of the cross and its personal application; or else it borders on blasphemy of the sinner's own response becomes part of the structure of objective atonement itself.

Denney, *The Death of Christ.* Incidentally, it is also the analogy preferred by both Barth and Brunner.[7]

(ii) By his resurrection our Lord establishes the victory (*nikē*) of God. The resurrection is called a victory (I Cor. 15:54, 55). It is certainly a victory over sin as a power (Romans 6) and over death as the final judgment of sin (I Cor. 15:56-57). Being the victory of God over sin and death it then takes its place with the atoning death as the foundation for the glorification of the believer.

(iii) By his priestly ministry our Lord keeps his people in the state of redemption. The intercessory ministry of our Lord is suggested in the great prayer of John 17 — note v. 9, "I am praying for them." It is referred to twice by Paul (Rom. 8:34, I Tim. 2:5), once by John (I John 2:1) and extensively in the letter to the Hebrews. From the time of the ascension until the time of his second appearing (Heb. 9:28) our Lord is our effective high priest at the right hand of God. Hebrews 7:25 states as clearly as any text in Hebrews that the intercessory ministry of Christ is unfailing, i.e., all whom he has redeemed through his sacrificial death he keeps in faith by his continuous intercession based upon the power of an endless life.

The echatological scope of this intercession is indicated in Hebrews 9:28, namely that he shall continue as an efficacious high priest until the day that he shall return to bring his redemption to perfection. The connection here with glorification is important. It is the intercessory ministry of Christ which preserves his people from justification until the time of their glorification.

SECTION 20: *The foundation of glorification in the application of the work of Christ to the believer*

The work of Christ objectively considered is the foundation of what he shall do in the future glorification of the believers. Correspondingly, the work of Christ as applied to the believer is the basis for the future glorification of the believer.

7 Leon Morris's *The Apostolic Teaching of the Cross* is a recent defense of the juridical interpretation of the atonement which employs the most recent materials in exegesis and biblical theology.

(i) We must note first of all the eschatological character of our salvation.[8] Our salvation is called a *promise* (*epagelia*). We are sealed with the Spirit of promise (Eph. 1:13); we have the promise of eternal life (I John 2:25, Tit. 1:2); the kingdom is promised to those who love him (Jas. 2:5); Christians are the recipients of the great promises of God (II Pet. 1:4); and saints of both the Old and New dispensations await together the fulfillment of the divine promises (Heb. 11:13, 39). In a word, what God does *now* is but a promise of the great things he shall do hereafter.

Our salvation is also called a *first fruits* (*aparxe*), for it is the beginning of that which shall eventually become the great harvest. Thus Christ as the first fruits of those that are fallen asleep (I Cor. 15:20, 23) is the promise of the resurrection-harvest of all of God's children. Christians are those who possess the first fruits of the Spirit (Rom. 8:23) as the anticipation of the great future harvest of redemption which shall be theirs in their glorification.

Besides being called a promise and a first fruits, our salvation is, thirdly, called an *earnest* (*arrobōn*). An *arrobōn* is a partial payment, a first installment, a deposit, a pledge which is a sample of what shall be delivered and also the obligation to make final and total delivery.[9]

Fourthly, it is called a *sealing* (*sphagis*). A sealing is the marking of something to hold it for final delivery.

Finally, it is called an *inheritance* (*klēronomia*) which shall be delivered over at the set time of inheritance.

In these five Greek words describing our salvation the eschatological character of our salvation is clearly seen. Our present salvation is a small beginning, and only a beginning, of things that will be accomplished in the age to come. Our glorification coincides with the completion of our salvation

8 Religious liberalism reduced eschatology to (i) the gradual extension of the kingdom of God as an ethical society, and (ii) the immortality of the soul. But much recent theology has recovered the more biblical perspective of eschatology. For the history of the subject in our century cf. Walter Kreck, *Die Zukunft des Gekommenen.* Cf. also Heinrich Ott, *Eschatologie* (*Theologische Studien*, Heft 53). Pierre Maury, *Eschatologie. Eschatology* (*Scottish Journal of Theology*, Occasional Papers No. 2).

9 Cf. *TWNT*, I, 474.

at the end-time initiated by the return of Christ. Nor should the eschatological character of the work of the Holy Spirit go unnoticed, for in virtually every one of these words it is the Holy Spirit who applies the seal and keeps the believer to the end-time.[10]

(ii) The individual acts of our now-salvation are eschatological in character. Justification is eschatological in that it anticipates the complete vindication of the believer in the end-time (Rom. 5:9-10). Regeneration is eschatological in that it anticipates the time when all things shall be made new, the palingenesis of all things. The word *palingenesia* is used for our present new-birth (Tit. 3:5) but also for the re-birth of all things.[11] Sanctification is eschatological in that it looks forward to the perfection of all things.[12] That which sums up the eschatological realization and fulfillment of our justification, our regeneration, and our sanctification is our end-time glorification.

10 Cf. Neil Hamilton, *The Holy Spirit and Eschatology in Paul.*

11 *TWNT*, I, 685ff. *Palingenesia* is parallel to "in my kingdom" and "in the coming age." Cf. also Rev. 21:5, "And he who sat upon the throne said, 'Behold, I make all things new.'"

12 Cf. the *apokatastasis* (to restore things to perfection) of Acts 3:21 and the *anakephalaioō* (to bring things to their culmination in Christ) of Eph. 1:10.

V The Glorification of the Soul

SECTION 21: *The glorification of the soul involves its perfection*

Up to this point we have attempted to establish the following theses: The Old and New Testaments teach (i) that God is a God of glory, (ii) that Jesus Christ is the Lord of Glory, (iii) that God intends to share his glory with his children in the form of their glorification, and (iv) that our present salvation, already begun, is a process which shall terminate in end-time, eschatological glory. We now turn in this and the following chapters to the details of this final glorification.

Salvation can be studied in the New Testament according to several themes. One of the more neglected one is the concept of perfection. This involves a number of similar words in the Greek language (*telos, teleiōtes, teleiōsis, teleō, teleios*). One of the reasons that there is so little constructive material on perfection is that the literature on the subject bogs itself down in debates over the degree of sanctification attainable in this life. Accordingly, the theme of perfection as a motif for salvation and as a strong eschatological concept are neglected.[1]

The perfection motif can be briefly sketched as follows. God intends a goal (*telos*) for his people. This goal involves the perfection (*teleios*) of the individual believer. But this calls for a Perfecter (*teleiōtēs*) who himself must undergo per-

---

1 A survey of encyclopedia articles will reveal that most of them do not discuss perfection as a motif of salvation nor as an eschatological concept. However, in P. J. Du Plessis, *Teleios, The Idea of Perfection in the New Testament,* we have an adequate treatment of perfection. Fr. Frerichs, however, recognizes the eschatological element in perfection in his article, "Vollkommenheit," *Evangelisches Kirchenlexikon,* III, 1700.

fecting and so become perfect (teleiōtheis). Thereby he can perfect (teloō) those who come unto God with a perfection (teleios). In this life perfection means spiritual, moral, and doctrinal maturity, but in the life to come it means perfection in the sense of the completion of salvation. The divinely intended purpose (telos) comes thereby to its consummation.[2]

The doctrine of perfection can accordingly be summed up in three theses: (i) Christ, having been perfected in virtue of his own experience, is the Perfecter of believers and also their perfection. (ii) In this life Christ formally gives us his perfection but calls us on to Christian maturity. (iii) In the age to come maturity gives way to full-orbed perfection. This is part of the structure of glorification and in this sense perfection and glorification coincide.

(i) Looking to the first of these theses we note the perfection of Jesus Christ. This is the theme uniquely developed in Hebrews. Spicq writes: "The entire epistle to the Hebrews attempts to prove the perfection of the New Covenant by the perfection of its high priest who procures perfection for his believers."[3]

Thus Christ is the Leader (arxēgos) of believers, for he first attains perfection. Hebrews 2:10 calls him the Perfected Leader. He attained this perfection by submitting to the conditions of our existence (Heb. 2:14-18), suffering the deepest lessons of obedience (Heb. 5:7-10) and finally suffering death itself. Risen from the dead he appears as the perfect fulfillment of all that the Old Testament promised. He is the perfect Moses, the perfect Aaron, the perfect minister in the perfect temple, the perfect sacrifice for sin, and the perfect Saviour for all who come unto God by him.

(ii) The second thesis asserts that Christ bestows his perfection upon those who believe. Hence in this life his bestowed perfection is equivalent to salvation (sotēria, Heb. 2:10, 5:9). In this sense Christ is the perfection of believers. As Frerichs

2 The book of Hebrews is the only book of the New Testament in which this is developed. Cf. Du Plessis, op. cit., pp. 206-232, and C. Spicq, L'Épitre aux Hébreux, I, 64, and II, 214.

3 Op. cit., I, 64.

emphasizes, Christ, the perfect One, is secretly present in the believer and in the Church as their hidden perfection.[4]

In leading us to glory Christ invites us to maturity in our own Christian experience. This is the burden of several New Testament passages. But it must be kept in mind that in each of these passages there is an eschatological arrow, for the present maturing anticipates the future perfecting. For this reason such passages suggest something of the character of final glorification.

"I in them and thou in me, that they may become perfectly one" (John 17:23). This is a plea for the perfection of unity. That this should be the effort of the church now cannot be denied. Paul exhorts the Ephesians to maintain the unity of the Spirit (Eph. 4:3). But the fragmentized nature of the church indicates how far the church has remained from perfect unity. Only in the end-time, in the glorification of the Church, will this unity emerge as perfected.[5]

"But when the perfect comes the imperfect will pass away," (I Cor. 13:10). The perfect (teleios) is contrasted with the partial (meros). The passage speaks of the mature gifts succeeding the childish (nēpios) gifts, but also of the perfection of the world to come succeeding the partial and limited character of our present experience. This is evident in verse 12, which speaks of our knowing with a fullness which corresponds to the fullness of God's knowledge of us. Du Plessis says that the emphasis is not on the mere partial character of our knowledge but upon the fragile character of our organs of perception compared to what they shall be in the future world.[6] Glorification in this connection means, then, proceeding from faculties and gifts which are partial to those which are perfect.[7]

"Having begun in the Spirit, are you now ending with the flesh?" (Gal. 3:3). In this verse to begin something is opposed to completing (epiteleō) something. If the latter verb is taken in the middle voice it means — as the Revised Standard

4. Op. cit., III, 1700. Cf. Du Plessis, op. cit., pp. 167-168.

5 Du Plessis, op. cit., p. 174.

6 Ibid., p. 185.

7 "This [perfection] is brought about at the parousia — it 'comes' with the Lord from heaven." EGT, II, 900. So also TWNT, IV, 600.

Version translates it — to end up with an attempt at sanctification in the flesh. If it is taken in the passive it means to be perfected in the flesh. Du Plessis[8] believes that the sense of the verb is passive. The verse speaks of a beginning and a completion. He thus translates the verse, "you were put under way by the Spirit, must the flesh now complete it?" Suffice it to say that the beginning of salvation in the Spirit is perfected by the same Spirit in the glorification of the end-time.

"And his gifts were that some should be apostles, some prophets, some evangelists, some pastors and teachers, for the equipment of the saints, for the work of ministry, for building up the body of Christ, until we all attain to the unity of the faith and of the knowledge of the Son of God, to mature manhood, to the measure of the stature of the fulness of Christ" (Eph. 4:1-13). This is a most remarkable passage in that it sets forth the goals of the divers ministries in the church. These goals are the perfecting of the saints, the work of the ministry, and the edification of the body of Christ. But these goals in turn have goals! These goals are the attainment by all of the unity of the faith, the profound knowledge (*epignōsis*) of the Son of God, the complete (*teleios*) man, and the mature stature measured by the fullness of Christ.

Several features stand out in this passage. The first is the forward motion in salvation. Faith must move steadily towards perfection and fullness. The second is the predominant physical imagery. Salvation proceeds, like the human body, from infancy (*nēpios*) to manhood (*anēr*). Hence the momentum of faith is not kinetic as in a rolling ball but as in a growing body. The third is the richness of this growth-imagery. It is the attainment of a goal; it is the acquiring of intimate knowledge; it is the perfection of manhood; and it is a fullness measured by the perfection of Christ. This fourfold standard will come into absolute fullness (as far as human nature is concerned) in the end-time glorification of the believer. The goal will be perfectly attained, the knowledge will be face-to-face knowledge, the manhood will be unqualified perfection, and the fullness will be fullness in its totality.

8 *Ibid.*, pp. 130-131.

"Not that I have already obtained this or am already perfect; but I press on to make it my own, because Christ Jesus has made me his own. . . . Let those of us who are mature be thus minded," (Phil. 3:12, 15). Here again we note a momentum. The first movement of the chapter is an account of Paul's moral and spiritual excellence as a Jew. The second movement is the great transition to faith in Christ and his righteousness. The third movement is the tremendous drive to come to the full realization of that which the gospel contains and offers. This third movement is intensely a *now* and *then* movement, or a *present-life* and an *eschatological* realization. It is a profound present knowing of Christ which anticipates the resurrection (vv. 10-11). It is an attempt to grasp Christ with the same intention with which Christ grasped us. It is a driving at the fastest pace to reach the finish line and receive the prize (vv. 13-14). The spiritual intensity of the passage is overpowering.

Those who are so intensely minded are the mature (*teleios*), and what they strive for is a perfection which is denied them in this life. The eschatological realization of the goals of this passage coincides with the glorification of the believer at the end-time.

"That we may present every man mature in Christ" (Col. 1:28). As Du Plessis indicates, the character of redemption is a dynamic moving from a beginning (*arxē*) of faith in Christ to the goal (*telos*) which is the final eschatological perfection (*teleios*).[9] This goal, we would add, is included in the more comprehensive act of our final glorification in and by Christ.

(iii) Third, we see perfection as an act of God in the age to come. Spicq says that to perfect somebody is to render that person perfect (*teleiosis*), and the perfection is the achievement of the goal (*telos*) of the person. Thus God perfects the Christian with the perfection which corresponds to God's *telos* in salvation.[10] Du Plessis affirms that the goal of perfection is the soteriological and eschatological work of Jesus Christ, the Messiah.[11]

9 *Ibid.*, p. 200.
10 *Op. cit.*, II, 214.
11 *Op. cit.*, p. 167.

Two references in Hebrews use perfection in this sense. "Since God had foreseen something better for us, that apart from us they should not be made perfect" (11:40); ". . . to the spirits of just men made perfect" (12:23). It must be admitted that Hebrews 11:40 could mean the perfection which Christ brought. In this sense it would mean that the benefits of Christ were withheld from the believers during the Old Testament until the coming of Christ. Or, it could refer to the end-time when the perfection of all things occurs. Hebrews 12:23 refers to the transformation undergone by the believers of the Old Covenant as they entered the glorious world described in Hebrews 12:22-24.

The intention of all these verses is obvious. The newborn Christian in this life is to press on to maturity. But the maturity of this life will always be partial. In the end-time glorification the imperfect maturity of this life will give way to the fullness of perfection.

SECTION 22: *The glorification of the soul involves its final vindication and moral perfection.*

(i) Paul has written that those whom God justifies he glorifies. This suggests strongly that glorification is the final realization of justification. Thus justification is at root eschatological, namely, the present justification of the believer will be consummated in end-time glorification.[12] The present vindication of the believer in Jesus Christ will then receive a final, perfect, and eternal vindication.

There are two passages in particular which discuss this end-time vindication, namely, Romans 5:9-10 and Romans 8:31-39. In Romans 5 we have a powerful treatment of the atonement in its fullest reaches. Christ died for the helpless, the ungodly, the sinners, and the enemies of God. This was a *vicarious* death, as is seen in the repeated use of the preposition "for"

12 For the eschatological intensity of justification see Richardson, *An Introduction to the Theology of the New Testament,* p. 237. R. Bultmann, *Theology of the New Testament,* I, 273f. G. Quell and G. Schrenk, "Righteousness," in *Kittel's Bible Key Words* (translated and edited by J. R. Coates).

(*huper*).[13]   The total impress of the passage is that Christ
does something for sinners which they cannot do for themselves.   His death manifests the love of God (v. 8), provides
justification (v. 9), and effects reconciliation (vv. 10-11).   This
justification and reconciliation is the present blessing of the
believer.   But Paul extends the virtue of the death of Christ
and the justification to the end-time.   The vicarious atoning
death represented here by the word *blood* (v. 9)[14] which *now*
justifies us will *then* save us from the wrath of God.   The
wrath of God is the holiness of God excited by the sinfulness
of man.   The death of Christ before the righteousness of God
(Rom. 3:25) enables God to be just in the justification of the
ungodly (Rom. 3:26).   This *present* justification results in
present freedom from condemnation (Rom. 8:1).   But in
the end-time when the wrath of God must make a final and
eternal reckoning with mankind's sins the believers shall not
be counted in.   Paul argues from the greater to the lesser.
If the death of Christ could vindicate us in the present age
from the absolutely wretched condition we were in, it shall
have no trouble with our final vindication before the wrath
of God.

Paul continues.   The death of Christ is also our present
reconciliation (Rom. 5:10).   Again Paul moves from the
greater to the lesser.   If the death of Christ could reconcile
us to God in our present wicked condition of enmity, the
intercessory life of Christ at God's right hand shall thoroughly
and completely save us from the wrath of God.

In Romans 8:31-39 the same theme of final vindication is
discussed from a different perspective.   The great affirmation
of Paul is that God is for us.   God has made our cause his
cause.   God seeks not first our condemnation but our justification.   If God is for us nothing can be against us (v. 31).   Then

13 Although *huper* fundamentally means "for the benefit of," it also
means, "in the place of."   There are some things which can be done for
another person's benefit only by doing it in his place, hence vicariously.
Therefore in many instances *huper* is equivalent to *anti*.   There are many
instances of this in the papyri.   Cf. Arndt and Gingrich, *A Greek-English
Lexicon of the New Testament*, p. 846.

14 "Blood and life as an expiatory sacrifice . . . as the means of freeing
from guilt."   Arndt and Gingrich, *op. cit.*, p. 22.

Paul again employs a logical principle. If God did such an enormous thing as to spare not his Son but deliver him up to death for us, then he will grace us with all things. Here the eschatological overtone enters. This promise does not refer so much to our earthly lives as to the matchless benevolence of God towards us in the end-time.

Speaking again of the present vindication of believers, Paul says that no man can successfully bring a charge against God's elect (v. 33). No man can dare condemn whom God has justified. Our vindication rests not in us as such, but in the past death of Christ for us and in the present intercession of Christ for us (v. 34). Our past justification and our present exoneration are secured for us by the love of Christ. But this love is so great that it shall be our guard for all the future, including the end-time. This is seen in such expressions as "neither death nor life" and "nor things to come" (v. 38). Therefore the believer stands completely secure in the love of Christ and his glorification as complete vindication at the end-time.[15]

(ii) The New Testament not only represents our glorification as a complete juridical exoneration but also as a moral perfection. This is revealed by the naming of certain moral qualities which will be bestowed upon believers at the return of Christ or at the end-time. Some of the more important moral qualities are:

Amōmos.[16] A *mōmos* was a fault, or a cause for blame, or a reason for censure. To be *amomōs* means to be free from such fault or blame. *Mōmos* was used also to indicate a spot or a blemish in a sacrificial animal. An animal without blemish was called *amōmos*. For example, the writer to the Hebrews calls Christ a perfect sacrifice (Heb. 9:14; see also I Pet. 1:9). The sense of spotting is seen in II Peter 2:13, where evil men are moral blemishes in the Christian fellowship whereas the Church when perfected and glorified

15 Cf. I Thess. 1:10, "Jesus who delivers us from the wrath to come," and references to white robes in Revelation (6:11, 7:9, 13, 14), and to white linen (15:6) or raiment (4:4, 19:8, 14, 3:5, 6, 18). White is the eschatological color and signifies glory, the radiance, and the righteousness of the wearers of the white garments.

16 *TWNT*, IV, 835-836.

(*endoxos*) by God will be without a moral blemish or spot (*amomōs*, Eph. 5:27).

The complete moral faultlessness[17] of the believer and the Church at the end-time is seen in the use of the verb "to present" with *amōmos* (Col. 1:22, Jude 24). We are so morally perfected that we may be presented to God completely faultless, spotless, and free from all censure. The same thought is present in Ephesians 1:4. Thus to be glorified is to be rendered *amōmos*. This is brought out in Jude 24, where in our faultlessness we can be "presented before the presence of his glory with rejoicing." If we were blameworthy it could be a presentation only with lament.

Hagios. Paul represents the believers as both blameless (*amōmos*) and holy (*hagios*) before God (Eph. 1:14, Col. 1:22). The concept of the holy is certainly one of the most complex and important in Scripture.[18] The God of both the Old and New Testaments is holy in that he is morally perfect. Negatively speaking, there is no darkness in him (I John 1:5, *oudemia* — "not at all, by no means"). To attribute anything morally imperfect to God is unthinkable, inconceivable and blasphemous. God is holy, his Son is holy, and his Spirit is holy. In the final assessment of all things only the holy can endure and be with God in eternity. The unclean or unholy is forever banished from his presence (Rev. 21:27, 22:15). No unholy person may take one small step into the New Jerusalem.

Our glorification in Christ involves, then, our being rendered holy to the degree that we perfectly satisfy the holiness of God; then our presence in the New Jerusalem will be completely free from all offense.

Aproskopos.[19] This word is derived from *proskoptō*. Its literal meaning is "to strike against something, to beat against, to stumble," and its figurative meaning is "to take offense at, feel repugnance for." From this verb two nouns are derived. *Proskopē* means an occasion for taking offense (II Cor. 6:3), and *proskomma* means a stumbling or occasion for stumbling.

17 In the LXX *amōmos* stands for the complete blamelessness of Yahweh. Cf. *TWNT*, IV, 836.

18 Cf. TWNT, I, 87-116, especially, "6. Die Ecclesia triumphans," pp. 111-112.

19 *TWNT*, VI, 745-759.

Aproskopos is thus an absence of offensiveness. It means to be free from cause of stumbling. In Philippians 1:10 Paul prays that Christians will be *aproskopos* in the day of Christ. The end-time reference here is unmistakable. Stählin[20] discusses three possibilities here. The word either means blamelessness, or without offence to God, or having reached the goal. Stählin prefers the latter, although the possibilities mentioned are not starkly opposed to each other. In the day of the believer's glorification he shall be completely without offense before God and his entry into the heavenly kingdom shall cause none to take offense for all such causes will have been removed from him.

Eilikrinēs. In Philippians 1:10 Paul associates *eilikrinēs* with *aproskopos.* This word has an interesting derivation.[21] It means to be tested by the sun; thence it means to be completely clear or pure or spotless and immaculate. In the day of Christ believers shall be tested by the sunlight and not be found wanting. Their glorification shall bestow upon them an immaculate purity which shall stand up under the eyes of him whose eyes burn like a flame of fire (cf. Rev. 1:4, 2:18, 19:12).

Anegklētos. This word, like so many words in this context, is formed by negating a word with a bad ethical meaning. *Egkaleō* means to bring a charge against somebody. The legal character of the word is seen in the remarks made by the town clerk in Ephesus (Acts 19:38, 40), the letter of Claudius Lysius to Felix (Acts 23:28, 29), and in Paul's speech before Agrippa (Acts 26:2, 6). The verb also occurs in Romans 8:33 where Paul asks if anybody can bring a charge against God's elect.

To be *anegklētos* means, then, to be free from an incriminating charge.[22] In the Pastorals it means that the servants of Jesus Christ are to be free from any civil charge, but in I Corinthians 1:8 it refers to the end-time status of Christians.[23]

20 *Ibid.,* p. 757.
21 *TWNT,* II, 396.
22 *TWNT,* I, 358.
23 Grundmann is strongly against Haupt at this point, for Haupt wishes to make these verses refer to the present life. *TWNT,* I, 358.

They stand before God completely free from any charge. According to Romans 8:31-34, when God justifies no man dare accuse. When Christ dies for sinners and intercedes for them there is no ground left for condemnation. In this realization of our salvation through glorification the Christian is rendered completely free from all moral objections.

Amemptos. This word is similar to *amōmos,* but it is not as strong a juridical word as *anegklētos.* It is derived from *memphomai* which means "to find fault with, blame, censure, etc." *Amemptos* means to be without fault, blame or censure. It is used of the excellent moral and religious behavior of men in this life (Zechariah and Elizabeth in Luke 1:6; Christians in Phil. 2:15; Paul's life prior to his conversion in Phil. 3:6; and his life as an apostle in I Thess. 2:10).

In I Thessalonians 3:13 and 5:23 the word has an eschatological meaning. These passages set forth ethical blamelesssness as the chief characteristic of our sanctification. According to the first, our hearts are to be found free from all fault before the Father at the return of Jesus Christ. In the second, Paul sets out the completeness of our sanctification by using two Greek words which express totality or thoroughness. This through-and-through sanctification involves the entire man — spirit, soul, and body. The product of this thorough sanctification is end-time blamelessness. The surety of this blamelessness is immediately attributed to God — "He who calls you is faithful, and he will do it" (v. 24). Thus our glorification involves our perfect faultlessness before God in the end-time appearing of Jesus Christ.

Spilos and *rhutis.* In Ephesians 5:25-27 Paul discusses how Christ shall perfect the Church. His sacrificial death enables him to sanctify and cleanse the Church, so that finally he might present the Church to himself gloriously (*endoxos*). This *endoxos* is elaborated by four other words, two of which we have already examined (*hagios* and *amōmos*). The other two words specify what the church is free from in her glory, namely, *spilos* (spot, stain, blemish) and *rhutis* (wrinkle, a wrinkle from old age). There is the subtle overtone here of the groom inspecting the bride for faults which destroy the physical perfection of the bride. But Christ shall morally perfect his church so that it shall be free from all moral spots and wrinkles. This is part of the glorification of Christians in the end-time.

SECTION 23: *The glorification of the soul involves its full participation in eternal life.*

The Old and New Testaments represent God as a living God (Deut. 5:26, Ps. 42:2, Matt. 16:16, Acts 14:15). The concept of God as the living God stems from two biblical motifs. The first is that as Creator God is also the Author of life; the second is that the God of Israel is the true God in contrast to the idols and gods of the pagans. The God of Israel is a living God whereas gods and idols are lifeless and powerless.

In the remarkable phrase of John 5:26 we are told that God has life in himself. He has uncreated life, life which has no beginning nor ending, and needing no sustenance. Barth says that to define God we must begin by saying that he is life. "Only the voice of the Living is God's voice. Only the work of the Living is God's work, only the worship and fellowship of the Living is God's worship and fellowship. So, too, only the knowledge of the Living is knowledge of God."[24]

Paralleling the statement of John 5:26 is I Timothy 6:16, which tells us that God is the only one possessing immortality (*athanasia*). Only God has this everlasting, uncreated life. This refers not only to the immutability and the eternity of the divine life, but also to its fullness and perfection.

It is in virtue of this divine life that created reality has life.[25] The living Elohim speaks in Genesis 1 and the earth *responds* with living forms. Life in the land, in the sea, and in the air stems from this living God. Whether it be vegetable or tree, creeping thing or cattle, it lives in virtue of the living God. The climax is the representation of man coming to life by the special spiration of God (Gen. 2:7). To this we may compare John's words when he wrote, "In him was life, and the life was the light of men" (John 1:4).

24 *Church Dogmatics*, II/1, p. 263.
25 "Life is represented [in the Old Testament] as a direct gift from God, and dependent absolutely upon Him for its continuance." J. J. Reeve, "Life," *ISBE*, p. 1888.

Man, in common with all living things, shares in life because the living God has given such life. But man is in the image and likeness of God and thereby shares a special, spiritual life. This is a gift to man above that of the other creatures. It is life as communion, as fellowship, as worship, as covenantal partnership with God. But as Scripture says repeatedly, this special life was forfeited by sin and turned into death. The breath of God in the nostrils of man makes him a living creature (Gen. 2:7), but disobedience is threatened with death just a few verses later (2:17). That the just end of sin is death (Rom. 6:23) is the common presupposition of both Testaments. Thus, as Bultmann points out, death for man in Scripture is never a "natural" event but is always viewed as a judgment of God upon sin.[26] The clearest passage on the unnatural character of death in its connection with sin is Romans 5:12-21.

The restoration of man's spiritual and divine life is represented as "life" or "eternal life."[27] There is no Platonism in the Scriptures, as if man's life were itself an immutable part of the eternal order.[28] Man's life finds its origin in God's gift, its forfeiture in man's sin, and its restoration through redemption, especially redemption seen as a new creation. This restoration is *in Christ*. In the great fifth chapter of John it is not only asserted that God has life in himself but also that the Son has life in himself (v. 26). Therefore the Son can execute two of God's absolute prerogatives: he can bestow upon the soul regenerate life in the present time (v. 24), and he can raise the dead at the last hour (vv. 21, 25, 28, 29).

Eternal life finds its first recovery in Christ as the living Son of God; it finds its second basis for recovery in Christ's resurrection from the dead.[29] Here again we note the absence of customary philosophical arguments. The entire future of

---

26 *TWNT*, III, pp. 14, 15. Cf. also Conzelmann, "Ewiges Leben," *RGG* (3), II, 804.

27 Cf. the excellent summary of M. S. Terry, "Eternal Life," *Dictionary of Christ and the Gospels*, I, 538-540. Terry has a real appreciation for the eschatological elements of the expression and its connection with glorification.

28 Conzelmann, *op. cit.*, p. 805.

29 So Bultmann emphatically in *TWNT*, II, 866.

man's body and soul, their end-time destiny, rests upon the person and work of Jesus Christ.[30]

The eternal life in Christ has three elements. It is first of all a new relationship. It is a knowing of the Father and the Son (John 17:3). It is therefore the restoration of the sinner to such a relationship with God that life is possible and truly does occur. But it is a restoration inseparable from Jesus Christ who is called the Author (*arxēgos*) of life[31] (Acts 3:15).

Secondly, eternal life is a new quality of life. It is a fellowship. The connection of eternal life and fellowship is seen in I John 1:1-3. It is the recovery of and participation in man's real life. Barth has described it as follows:

> The purpose of God in His judgment is the sanctification of man, i.e., his direction, preparation and exercise for the eternal life ordained and promised. Eternal life is a life which, ascribed to man in his creatureliness, is invested with God's own glory, i.e., as an object of the openly revealed love of God in which God has turned to him and in possession of the openly revealed freedom which He has granted him in fellowship with Himself. It is man's indissoluble, indestructible, unceasing and unlimited life with God, his life in the clarity which is proper to God, in which God sees Himself, in which He has always seen man, too, and still sees him but in which here and now man is so far unable to see either God or himself . . . . Eternal life is man's life in harmony with the life of God.[32]

Thirdly, eternal life is life into eternity. It is endless life. This is especially seen in the contrasts which are drawn. In II Timothy 1:10 it is contrasted with death; in Matthew 25:46 with eternal punishment; in John 3:16 with destruction; in John 5:24 with judgment and death.[33]

---

30 This is seen in II Tim. 1:10 where it is attributed to the gospel of Christ that it lightens up, i.e., reveals, life and immortality. E. F. Scott's very able article on "Life" (*Dictionary of Christ and the Gospels*, II, 30-32) nevertheless fails to grasp the radical theological, Christocentric, and eschatological character of eternal life. The interpretation is too moralistic and Ritschlian to do justice to the New Testament.

31 It could also be translated "Prince of Life," or "Leader of Life."

32 *Op. cit.*, II/2, pp. 772-773.

33 Althaus says that the opposite of eternal life is existence unto death (*Totsein*). RGG (3), II, 805.

The firm teaching of the New Testament is that eternal life is a present possession. The following verbs show how eternal life is now received: enter (Matt. 18:8); have (Matt. 19:16); inherit (Mark 10:17); receive (Mark 10:30); see (John 3:36). Therefore in this life eternal life as a relationship and as a quality of life is already begun and as such it is an earnest of eternity.[34] Althaus describes it as follows:

> So eternal life is for the Christian transcendent and at the same time his own possession, future and present, a secret of faith which will reveal itself in the future and faith yet already knows it at work here and now.[35]

This introduces us to the central issue: our glorification involves the full bestowal of eternal life upon the soul — a perfect relationship, a sublime quality, and an eternal duration. Thus the concept is through and through eschatological and redemptive.[36] For this reason Althaus says very emphatically that eternal life is not built on any doctrine of the continuity or durability of the soul. Such a concept is neutral with regard to salvation or damnation. The biblical doctrine of eternal life is grounded in salvation[37] and is thoroughly eschatological.[38]

SECTION 24:   *The glorification of the soul involves its full participation in the freedom of the sons of God*

The concept of freedom[39] in Scripture is rooted in the concept of the freedom of God. The traditional theological term which expresses the freedom of God is the sovereignty of God.

---

34 The fullness of the New Testament teaching about life is too great to reproduce here; e.g., there is a gate and a way which lead to life; there is the light of life; the inner spring of life; the abundance of life; the food of life; the words of life, etc. Cf. "*Zaō,*" *TWNT*, II, 831-877.

35 *Op. cit.*, p. 808.

36 Negatively speaking eternal life is to be saved; put positively it is entering into glory. So Bultmann, *TWNT*, II, 871.

37 Althaus calls it a *Heils-Begriff. Op. cit.*, p. 806.

38 *Ibid.*, p. 808.

39 J. P. Thornton-Duesbery, "Free, freedom, etc.," *A Theological Word Book of the Bible*, p. 87. E. Fahlbusch, "Freiheit," *EKL*, I, 1372-1379. R. Martin Pope, "Liberty (Christian)," *HERE*, VII, 907-911. E. Fuchs, "Freiheit," *RGG* (3), II, 1101-1104. H. Schlier, "*eleuthros,*" *TWNT*, II, 484-500.

To be sovereign is to be free to do what one wills. To be free in a real and final sense is to be sovereign. Although theologians have differed in the degree to which God expresses his sovereignty or in the manner in which God expresses it, nevertheless they are uniform in ascribing freedom and sovereignty to God.

The concept of the freedom of God is one of the basic axioms of Barth's theology. No theologian in the history of theology has treated the topic so extensively and in so many divisions of systematic theology.[40] The freedom of God is the root and foundation for all freedom for the creature. God's freedom is, first, negative: it is complete freedom from limits, restrictions, and conditions.[41] But second and more important is the positive element in God's freedom. In speaking of the positive side of freedom Barth writes:

> But freedom in its positive and proper qualities means to be grounded in one's own being, to be determined and moved by one's self. This is the freedom of the divine life and love. In this positive freedom of His, God is also unlimited, unrestricted and unconditioned from without. He is the free Creator, the free Reconciler, the free Redeemer . . . . He in Himself is power, truth and right. Within the sphere of His own being He can love and love in absolute plenitude of power, as we see Him in love in His revelation.[42]

It is out of God's own freedom that he wills to create a universe, that he wills to bring life into existence, and that he wills to form man as his supreme creature. It is out of this selfsame freedom that God wills to be the Lord and Partner of this man, that he wills to enter into communion with this man, and that he grants out of his own freedom a freedom for man to be the man before God. Thus man's freedom grows out of God's freedom, it is a gift of God's freedom, and he can exist as man within this special form of freedom.

40. E.g., *Church Dogmatics*, I/1 and I/2, discusses extensively the freedom of God in revelation. The intensive treatment of God's freedom is found in II/1, Section 28, Paragraph 3, "The Being of God in Freedom." When Barth discusses this in detail (in contrast to General Ethics of II/2) in conection with creation, he develops the entire theme around the concept of freedom as the gift of the Creator to the creature (III/4).

41 *Ibid.*, II/1, p. 301.

42 *Ibid.*

Deep in the history of theology is the conviction that man's freedom is not an abstract concept. It is not merely freedom to will or to choose, freedom to hew out one's own destiny, freedom to do one's own pleasure. When Augustine opened the *Confessions* by saying that man was made for God and could not rest until he rested in God he was affirming that man's freedom was a freedom to be realized in God. When Thomas said that God is man's beatitude he was asserting that the being of man was a being which could come to its fulfillment only in God. And if this is true of man's being as such it is also true of man's freedom.

We therefore come to the conclusion that freedom is a fundamental characteristic of man. To be free is to be the true man before the living God, to display the divine image. Freedom for man is therefore also to be the lord of creation (Gen. 1:28). Man is free to be the mate of woman, as she is free to be the helpmeet of man. Freedom means man's freedom to originate and order a society, and to live within the terms of grace and love in the divine covenant.

That day in which man attempted to live in any other terms than the terms of his freedom would be the day man would die (Gen. 2:17). Sin terminates the fullness of this freedom. The presupposition of Scripture is that man is in bondage — a thesis expressed in a thousand different ways. Therefore the great emphasis in the New Testament is not about freedom as such or even the original freedom of man but upon the freeing of man.[43]

Man, as a sinner, is in bondage. If freedom is the sign of sinlessness under the perfect law of Edenic existence, then bondage (*douleia*) is the sign of his sinnerhood. Thus man is a slave (*doulos*) enslaved (*douleuō*) in slavery (*douleia*).

The wonderful witness of the New Testament is that Christ redeems man from his slavery. When our Lord commenced his ministry and gave his famous address to the synagogue in Nazareth he said in citing Isaiah that he would "proclaim release to the captives" (Luke 4:18). This is certainly a great theme of the Christian gospel.

43 Cf. E. Fahlbusch, *op. cit.*, p. 1374. *TWNT*, II, 492.

The great bondage-freedom section of Scripture is Romans 6. Man is represented as enslaved to sin (v. 6), under the dominion of death (v. 9), under the reign of sin (v. 12), under the law (v. 14), a slave of sin (vv. 16, 17, 20), and free from righteousness (v. 20). That which smites the chains of sin, the law, and death, providing release and freedom, is the death and resurrection of Jesus Christ. As Schlier[44] points out, it is the complete self-surrender of Christ to a vicarious death which is the basis for our freedom.

Romans 6 also illustrates the character of the biblical doctrine of freedom. Man's freedom is not fulfilled in the complete freedom from restraint to act as he pleases. It is the freedom of the new life in Christ (v. 4); it is to live free from sin (v. 7); it is to be alive to God in Jesus Christ (v. 11); it is yielding one's self as risen men are yielded (v. 13); it is to be under grace (v. 14); it is to be slave of righteousness (v. 18); it is to be rewarded with sanctification in this life and eternal life in the end-time (v. 22). Thus Thornton-Duesberry is correct when he writes that "Christian freedom is part and parcel of the new order of things inaugurated by God in Jesus Christ."[45]

The book of Galatians is in complete harmony with Romans 6. The bondage of man due to his sinfulness is overcome in the life, death, and resurrection of Jesus Christ. By taking the curse of the law upon himself (Gal. 3:13) Christ ends our bondage and secures our liberty (5:1).

The freedom lost in sin, rescued again by the redemption of Jesus Christ, is now, in this age, bestowed upon the believer. Freedom in Christ is one of the greatest blessings of our present salvation in Christ.[46] If the death and resurrection of Christ is the historical foundation of our freedom (as Rom.

---

44 *TWNT*, II, 495.

45 *Op. cit.*, p. 87. "Throughout the New Testament liberty (*eleutheria*) and its even more confident form (*exousia*) runs as a golden thread, distinguishing the New Dispensation from the Old." E. Daplyn, "Liberty," *Dictionary of Christ and the Gospels*, II, 29.

46 Bultmann lists freedom as one of the four major characteristics of the man under faith. *Theology of the New Testament*, I, Chapter V.

8:3 indicates), the present in-this-life foundation is the Holy Spirit of God.[47] The important passages which speak directly of the Holy Spirit as the immediate source of Christian freedom are: Romans 8:3-27, II Corinthians 3:17, Galatians 3:3, 14, 4:5-7, 5:5, 16, 18, 22, 25, 6:8. It is the Spirit who accomplishes directly and concretely in Christian experience the freedom we have in Christ.[48] These freedoms are:

(i) Freedom from sin. Our Lord, speaking of the Christians, said, "the sons are free" (Matt. 17:26). The mark of the Christian is that Christ the Son sets the sons free from the dominion of sin (John 8:33-36). The truth does set free! But it is the truth about Jesus Christ the Son of God, not truth in general. Few biblical texts are more abused than John 8:33. The Son does not basically set free from superstition or ignorance but from sin. Christ the Redeemer calls us to freedom (Gal. 5:1, 13).

Freedom from sin (Rom. 6, 7, 8) does not mean freedom from temptation nor from never sinning again, but freedom from the compulsion to sin.[49] Thus John writes that the person who thinks that he does not sin is deceived (I John 1:8), yet Christians born of God do not sin (I John 3:4-9), i.e., do not live under the compulsive power of sin. They live under the law of the Spirit of life in Christ Jesus which frees them from the compulsion of the law of sin and death (Rom. 8:2). Paul contrasts spirit and flesh at this point. To walk in the Spirit is to walk in freedom from the compulsion of sin; to walk in the flesh is to live under the compulsion of

47 According to the same passage (Rom. 8:3) this present freeing power of the Spirit grows out of the work of Christ on the cross and in his resurrection. Cf. Schlier, op. cit., II, 495. Otto Weber, Grundlagen der Dogmatik, II, 288ff.

48 Bultmann says that by the Spirit Paul does not mean mysticism or ecstasy. "Rather, everything indicates that by the term 'Spirit' [Paul] means the eschatological existence into which the believer is placed by having appropriated the salvation deed that occurred in Christ." Op. cit., I, 335. "The primary idea [of Spirit] is that of the miraculous power of God, then, since it has the effect of emancipating from the power of sin and death — i.e., grants freedom of action and opens up the possibility of reaping eternal life — it is also the norm for 'walking.'" Ibid., I, 336.

49 Ibid., I, 332. Fahlbusch, op. cit., i, 1374.

sin (Rom. 8:1-8). Bultmann defines the relationship of spirit and flesh as follows:

> The Spirit is the opposite of 'flesh.' . . . As 'flesh' is the quintessence of the worldly, visible, controllable, and transitory sphere which becomes the controlling power over man who lives 'according to the flesh,' so 'Spirit' is the quintessence of the non-worldly, invisible, uncontrollable, eternal sphere which becomes the controlling power for and in him who orients his life 'according to the Spirit.' "[50]

(ii) Freedom from the deception of sin. Life in sin is a life of deception. This much is clear from John 9:39-41. That it is also life as a *lie* is the implication of John 8:39-47.[51] To exist in deception and in a lie is a most vicious form of bondage.

When Jesus Christ redeems he enables the sinner to recover himself from the deception and the lie of sin. He discovers himself as he *was* in virtue of what he now *is* in Christ. Christian freedom includes freedom from deception:[52] this is brought out in Paul's personal remarks in Philippians 3. Paul's life before conversion was really the life of Paul deceived. It was Paul in sin but deceived into thinking he was in righteousness. It was Paul full of fault before God but deceived into thinking that he was faultless. It was Paul in terrible disservice to God deceived into thinking that he served God with a holy zeal. But when Paul found Christ he also found himself, for in finding Christ he found freedom from deception. The whole bent of his life changed, for now the impetus in Paul's life was not to justify Paul but to know Christ.

iii) Freedom from the law. Paul represents the bondage of the law in a twofold manner. First, it is bondage to a false method of salvation. It presumes that man can establish his own righteousness (Rom. 10:3, Phil. 3:1-6). Second, it is bondage to a false method of sanctification. It presumes that in the keeping of the law there is growth in sanctification (Gal. 3:1-5). The great theme of freedom from the law is discussed in Romans, Galatians, and II Corinthians 3.

---

50 *Op. cit.*, I, 334.
51 Schlier, *TWNT*, II, 493.
52 *Ibid.*, II, 494.

The details of this great antithesis of bondage under the law and freedom in Christ are too many for a thorough treatment here. The law is holy, just, and good (Rom. 7:12). But it is commandment and not gospel. Its broken statutes bring a curse (Gal. 3:13) and guilt (Jas. 2:10). It is written on the slate of stone and not upon the human heart. It rests its heavy demands upon a sinful heart. The sinful heart responds adversely to the law and thus the law excites dormant sinful propensities (Rom. 7:7-12). It was given to direct life (Rom. 7:10) but it cannot bestow life for it is commandment and not promise (Gal. 3:21). Therefore for wicked sinners it turns out to be a ministration of death and damnation (II Cor. 3:7-9).

Christ died to redeem us from the curse of the law (Gal. 3:13), nailing its charges against us on the cross (Col. 2:4). We are then dead to the law (Rom. 7:4) and discharged from the law (Rom. 7:6). We now live in the freedom of the Holy Spirit, for where the Spirit of the Lord is, there is liberty (II Cor. 3:17). We are free from the whole sacrificial system of the Old Testament, for it is shadow and Christ is reality (Col. 2:17). We are free from attempting to justify or sanctify ourselves by the law. We are free from the seal and sign of the law — circumcision. We are free from all the rules, regulations, and institutions of the law. We are free to live under the perfect law of freedom (Jas. 1:25). We are free to be "inlawed" to Christ (I Cor. 9:21). We are free to live as free men (I Pet. 2:16). We are free from all the veiled and disguised forms of legalism.[53] We are free from all the standards and conventions of men so that we might be our true selves in Jesus Christ.[54]

(iv) Freedom from idolatry and world systems. In Galatians Paul goes beyond freedom from the law. We are children of the free woman (Gal. 4:31) and in this freedom from the bondage of the law we are to stand firmly (Gal. 2:4, 5:1, 13). But Paul makes it clear that idolatry is a form of bondage (Gal. 4:8). The true knowledge of God frees the believer from this bondage (Gal. 4:9).

53 *Ibid.*, II, 493.
54 Fahlbusch, *op. cit.*, I, 374.

Paul also sees the whole pagan religious life as a form of bondage (Gal. 4:9-10, Eph. 2:2). To be in Christ is to be free from the fear, the superstition and the regulations of pagan religion in all its forms. Thus in Colossians 2:8 he warns the Christians against being taken prey by powerless philosophy, human tradition, and the elemental spirits of the universe. In Colossians 2:18 he warns against self-abasement and worship of angels. In Colossians 2:16 he sounds a clear note of Christian freedom from all pagan religion — "let no man pass judgment on you!"

Again, in Colossians 2:20-3:4 Paul maintains the liberty we have in Christ against "the elemental spirits of the universe" (v. 20), against "regulations" (v. 20), against "human precepts and doctrines" (v. 22). The Christian's life is free from all of this in order that it might be free for the life in Christ.

(v) Freedom from death. Because the Christian is free from sin's compulsion and free from the bondage of the law he is free from the sting of death. Paul puts all three together in I Corinthians 15:56. The power of sin is the law; and death is the sting (*kentron,* the poisonous, deadly sting of the insect) of the law. The Christian is not exempt from the experience of dying but he is exempt from its sting. Having been united with the crucified and risen Lord he is passed beyond all the threat and terror of death.

Hebrews 2:14-18 is beautifully clear on this point. In our fear of death before we knew Christ we became willing prey to the religious systems of Satan and thus entered into his bondage. Christ comes, however, in our human nature, suffers our death, expiates our sins, and delivers us into the freedom of his great salvation.

The climax, fulfillment, and complete realization of our freedom in Christ is part of our glorification. This is the great theme of Romans 8:18-25 and II Corinthians 4:16-18. In Romans 8:18 Paul speaks of the present sufferings (*pathēma,* suffering, misfortune, of the redemptive sufferings of Christ) ;[55] and in II Corinthians 4:16 of the wasting away of the outer nature, which he calls in verse 17 "slight momentary afflictions"

---

55 H. Kittel, *Die Herrlichkeit Gottes,* p. 195.

(*thlipsis,* oppression, affliction, tribulation, distress). Added to these sufferings and these tribulations is the curse imposed on creation due to man's sin which Paul calls a frustration (*mataiotēs*) in Romans 8:20. The frustration inhibits the goal (*telos*) of creation from reaching its realization. This is compounded with the effects of the curse upon our bodies, for they too suffer from the frustration imposed upon the creation (Rom. 8:23). Therefore Christians groan inwardly, longing for the release from the frustrations of their spiritual life arising from hindrances from their bodies. This is again compounded with a fourth factor, namely, human weakness (*astheneia*) or spiritual frailty (Rom. 8:26). Insofar as our sufferings, our tribulations, our existence under frustration, and our weakness prevent our full and unhindered life as God's redeemed children, our present life is a life of bondage. *Therefore our glorification represents a total removal of all these restrictions, permitting the children of God to live in glorious freedom, to be fully conformed to what they truly are.*

Thus our eschatological freedom is freedom from sin, freedom from the law, freedom from death. It is freedom from suffering, frustration, and tribulation. But it is more than this; it is freedom to be true to our natures as God's children. Release from this bondage is entry into complete freedom and glory. Thus our glorification and our full freedom coincide. The former produces the latter. In Romans 8:21 Paul uses the unique expression "glorious freedom," i.e., freedom which is glorious. In II Corinthians 4:17 he speaks of the "eternal weight of glory" which shall be ours when we enter into those things which are eternal.

SECTION 25:   *The glorification of the soul is bestowed upon the soul when it enters into its full inheritance in Jesus Christ*

The biblical doctrine of inheritance[56] is founded in the promise made to Abraham, namely, that having left his father-

---

56 "*Klēros*," *TWNT*, III, 757-786. C. E. B. Cranfield, "Inherit, etc.," *Theological Word Book of the Bible*, pp. 112-114. B. S. Easton, "Heir," *ISBE*, 1369. A. J. Mclean, "Heir, etc.," *Dictionary of the Apostolic Church*, I, 534-544. *EGT*, III, 262-264. Paul Feine, *Theologie des Neuen Testaments* (8th edition), p. 228.

land he would be granted another country for the possession of his offspring. It received a more extensive development in the promises to Moses that those redeemed out of Egypt should enter into a land flowing with milk and honey, and was partially fulfilled in the conquest of Joshua. Milk and honey were luxury items with the ancients and a land *flowing* with such luxurious fare was certainly a land blessed of the Lord.

The Israelites were continually reminded, however, that they did not receive this inheritance because they deserved it.[57] It was not originally their rightful property, nor was it bequeathed to them in reward for national excellence. Furthermore, they did not conquer it by their own power even though they fought for it. It is everywhere regarded as a bestowal of the Lord, a grant of his grace and a continued possession in virtue of his grace, power, and will.

The more legally flavored concept of inheritance grows out of the need to partition the land through lot and thus to transmit it from father to son. But the concept of inheritance as gracious bestowal is more fundamental than and prior to the concept of inheritance as a rightful bequest.[58]

The concept of inheritance takes on a spiritual overtone in the Old Testament which foreshadows what will happen to it in the New Testament. The first overtone is suggested where we read that the Levites shall not have a lot of the land, for the Lord is their lot. The second overtone is seen in those passages where Israel is set forth as God's possession in the same sense as the land is God's possession or Israel's.[59] The third is to be found in Psalm 16:5-6, "The Lord is my chosen portion and my cup; thou holdest my lot. The lines have fallen for me in pleasant places." The Psalmist con-

---

57 "In the biblical language *klēronomia* is seen less as the acquisition of a property after the death of the first owner and more as the successor taking possession, and the word is thus employed more often for acquisition pure and simple, of the accession to lordship." C. Spicq, *op. cit.*, II, 5.

58 Even here the bequeathal of the lot of Israel to his heirs is not purely legal but based upon the fidelity and promise of the Lord. *TWNT*, III, 774. Cranfield notes that the Old Testament never connects Israel's lot (*nachalah*) with the father-son metaphor. *Op. cit.*, p. 113.

59 *TWNT*, III, 771.

trasts his portion in the Lord with the portion of those who have chosen idols (v. 4). He boldly applies terms used literally of the partition of the land into lots for his spiritual heritage in the Lord. The surveyor's lines which marked out the assigned lot[60] mark out the Lord as the pleasant place of the Psalmist.

The New Testament transposes the Old Testament concept of inheritance in certain significant ways. First, the heir is designated to be Jesus Christ.[61] This means that all inheritance will hereafter be mediated through this Heir. There is no inheriting apart from Christ (Gal. 3:29). Foerster thinks it is decisive that the Son of the parable of Mark 12:1-10 is also the Heir.[62] Equally decisive is Hebrews 1:3, which affirms that Christ is the Heir of all things.[63] Spicq comments as follows on Hebrews 1:3:

> It is remarkable that Jesus as only a man having belonged to one of the smallest nations of the world, which rejected and crucified him, has been established as heir not only of Palestine or the Orient, but of the universe, of all the riches of earth and heaven. He is the Lord and Master of all that exists.[64]

The inheritance was hidden during the earthly life of Christ. Only as the Risen Lord does he come into the full exercise of this lordship implied in being heir of all things.[65] As Gerhard Koch spells it out in such great detail and emphasis in his work, *Die Auferstehung Jesu Christi*, the Risen Christ appears to his disciples as THE LORD.[66]

The second transformation comes in the reinterpretation of the heirs of God. According to Foerster's account of Jewish theory, Abraham's heirs were his descendants and proselytes who kept the law.[67] But Paul, according to Foerster, modifies this concept in the light of four theses:[68] (i) The promise

---

60 F. Delitzsch, *A Commentary on the Book of Psalms*, I, 283.
61 *TWNT*, III, 781.
62 Foerster, *op. cit.*
63 The heir of all things means that Christ is the recipient of all things. B. S. Easton, *op. cit.*, p. 1369.
64 *Op. cit.*, II, 5.
65 *TWNT*, III, 782.
66 Cf. p. 41, "Ostern ist Auferweckung Jesu zum Kyrios."
67 *TWNT*, III, 784f.
68 *Ibid.*, pp. 784-785.

given to Abraham was given before the law and was received as a promise and not by fulfilling the law. (ii) Therefore the true sons of Abraham are those who have faith. (iii) The real seed of Abraham is one person, Jesus Christ. Therefore to be a seed of Abraham one must belong to Christ. This further displaces the keeping of the law as the ground for heirship. (iv) Paul reinterprets Abraham in the light of Christ and holy history. The real heir of Abraham, then, is the person who participates in holy history.

The third transformation comes in the addition of an eschatological note to the concept of inheritance.[69] What was promise in the Old Covenant becomes eschatological anticipation in the New Testament. There is eschatological anticipation in the Old Testament insofar as both Israel and the land are called God's heritage, which heritage is not based upon Israel's industry and business but upon God's gift.[70] But in the New Testament it clearly emerges that the concept of inheritance belongs not only to the present but also to the end-time (Acts 26:18, Col. 1:12).

The fourth transformation is seen in what is inherited (according to the New Testament). No longer is the object of inheritance the land[71] or Israel or the temple or the torah, but the kingdom or eternal life or salvation. According to Foerster the true perspective of the New Testament doctrine of inheritance is to be gained from Revelation 21:2-7. Here is the final realization of the end-time of the kingdom of God, of life, of salvation and of blessing.[72] The land-promise to Abraham has now gone through a complete transformation.[73]

Our inheritance in Christ is both present and future and

69 Spicq says that the concept of inheritance is a good messianic-eschatological one. *Op. cit.*, II, 5.

70 *TWNT*, III, 779.

71 *TWNT*, III, 782. Foerster interprets Matt. 5:5 as meaning the receiving of the riches of the Lordship of God. It is not a piece of earth or a piece of heaven that is inherited but the fullness of life under the divine lordship. Sasse points out the messianic-eschatological meaning of "inheriting the earth." *TWNT*, I, 676.

72 *TWNT*, III, 783.

73 "In the New Testament [inheritance] gets the higher sense of the blessedness of the Messianic kingdom, the Christian's destined possession in the consummation of the kingdom of God." Salmond, *EGT*, III, 263.

therefore its fullness is part of our glorification. Christians are heirs because they are sons. Paul uses a strong word, adoption (*huiothesia*), to indicate how believers are brought into the divine family (Gal. 4:5, Eph. 1:5, Rom. 8:15).[74] In Romans 8:17 Paul deduces the Christians' status as that of heirs from their status as sons; and from the status of heirship he deduces co-heirship with Christ. Virtually the same thing is affirmed in Galatians 3:6-7.

In analogy with Israel, believers are in turn called God's heritage. Peter thus calls the Christians God's possession (I Pet. 5:3, *hoi klēroi*).[75] Ephesians 1:14 may mean either that Christians are given an inheritance or that they have been made God's heritage. Salmond prefers the latter.[76] Ephesians 1:18 is more emphatic: "Having the eyes of your hearts enlightened, that you may know what is the hope to which he has called you, what are the riches of his glorious inheritance in the saints." Here is the clear union of eschatological hope and Christian inheritance.

Christians are represented as inheriting. They inherit (*klēronomeō*) as their lot (*klēros*) salvation or the kingdom of God or eternal life (Acts 26:18, Col. 1:12). They are thus said to have an inheritance (*klēronomia*). The *heir* who is given his *lot* and so *inherits* his *inheritance* comes into its fullness in the end-time, and thus his inheritance corresponds to the believer's glorification. That our full inheritance is yet future and corresponds with our glorification is expressed absolutely in Romans 8:17, 18, 23. Insofar as the inheritance is itself eschatological (the kingdom, I Cor. 6:9; eternal life, Matt. 19:29; eternal sonship, Rev. 21:7), the time of the inheriting must be the end-time. Peter clearly affirms that the living hope of the Christian is an imperishable, undefiled and unfading inheritance which is reserved in heaven by God for us and shall be revealed in that last day (I Pet. 1:3-5).[77]

---

74 Even this adoption is eschatological, as the adoption of the body corresponds with the end-time glorification of the believer (Rom. 8:23).

75 *TWNT*, III, 763 says this could mean the lots (i.e., congregations) assigned the bishops.

76 *EGT*, III, 263.

77 The future of inheriting is suggested in Col. 3:24, where it is associated with rewards; in Heb. 9:15, where our inheritance is called eternal;

In Titus 3:7 Paul connects justification, inheritance, and eternal life. In our justification we become heirs of an end-time bestowal of eternal life in its fullness, and this coincides with the Christian's glorification. By way of summary, then, the Christian's inheriting of his inheritance is an end-time event and an integral part of the glorification of the saints.

SECTION 26: *The glorification of the soul is its conformity to the spiritual image of Jesus Christ*

Jesus Christ is everywhere in the New Testament assumed to be the moral and spiritual ideal of the Christian. In his purity of life, perfect obedience to the Father, composure in the hour of persecution, steadfastness in suffering, and resistance to sin he is the model for the Christian when he enters into similar situations. In this life we strive to be like the Saviour; in our end-time glorification our souls shall be perfectly conformed to his image.

This conformity to Christ is the announced purpose of God as recorded in Romans 8:28-29. Christ is the first-born among the Christians. He is the elder Brother who is the pattern to which all the other brothers shall conform. But the hope here is eschatological and awaits the end-time fulfillment.[78] The image of the Son is not attained until the brothers have gone through the resurrection as has the elder Brother.[79]

This being our goal, we move in this life towards that goal, a goal which is on the other side of the resurrection. In Colossians 1:28 Paul speaks of his desire to present every man to Christ as mature in Christ. Christian maturity in this life finds its realization in conformity to Christ's perfect human nature in the world to come. This is taught more explicitly in Ephesians 4:13, a passage we discussed under the topic of perfection, but it is relevant simply to restate here that maturity and perfection have as their standard Christ-

---

in Eph. 1:14, where we are sealed with the Spirit as an earnest until we shall receive our inheritance.

78 Cf. "*prototokos*," *TWNT*, VI, 878.

79 Sanday and Headlam, *op. cit.*, take *prototokos* to mean eldest born.

likeness. Just as the unity of faith yields to end-time perfect unity, the knowledge of the Son of God yields to end-time complete knowledge, the manhood of the believer yields to the perfect image of the manhood of Christ at the end-time. Glorification is then the perfecting of our manhood into the image of the perfect human nature of Jesus Christ.

This is also the theme of Philippians 3:11-13, which was also discussed under the concept of perfection. But here, as in the Ephesians passage, the concept of perfection and the concept of conformity to the image of Christ overlap. In the Philippians passage Paul desires to *know* Christ in his suffering and in his resurrection, and certainly this *knowing* implies a *becoming like* Christ. Paul admits that he has not achieved the end of this knowing in this life (v. 12) but presses on towards it even though he knows it can only be fully achieved at the resurrection. Thus the goal is an eschatological goal since it can be fully realized only at the time of the resurrection, and it is a Christological goal because Paul wishes to grasp Christ so that he may become like him.

The most striking of those passages which refer to our becoming like Christ is II Corinthians 3:18. Just as Moses gazed on the glory of the Lord and his face shone with the glory of the Lord, so we look upon the Lord of glory and his glory radiates upon us. In this exposure to the glory of Christ we are transposed into the image or likeness (*eikōn*) of the Lord. But this is not a sudden change: it is from glory to glory, i.e., from degree to degree. Ultimately, when the transformation is complete, Christians will possess the complete image of Christ. And this amazing chemistry of personality transformation is effected by the Lord, the powerful Holy Spirit. We need only add that the final transformation into the image and glory of Christ corresponds with our glorification.

That this final transformation is eschatological and therefore belongs to the end-time is clear from I John 3:2. Although we undergo change in this life from glory to glory, the final change is at the appearing of Christ. We are now (*nun*) God's children, but there is no visible sign that distinguishes us from those who are not Christians. One cannot surmise the future state from the present condition. But in some future date it will be revealed. What we are now secretly shall become apparent. As God's children we are destined to become like God's Son. When he is revealed in his glory at his return, then we shall see him in his radiant glory and become as he is. Thus conformation to the perfect human nature of Jesus Christ coincides with glorification.

VI The Glorification of the Body

SECTION 27: *The nature of man in biblical perspective*

The glorification of man involves the total man. In the previous chapter we emphasized those aspects of glorification which were more centrally related to the soul or the total self or the person. In this chapter we emphasize the place of the body in glorification.

Especially in the light of recent biblical theology, it is beyond dispute that the Scriptural writers attribute a real dignity to the human body. This is evident, first of all, in the creation accounts (Gen. 1:26-30, 2:4-25), which express the dignity of man in a twofold manner. The first expression comes in the *special attention* given to the creation of man. In the first account he is placed as the last and highest of God's creations, and in the second account his formation is described in much greater detail than that of other created things. The second expression of this dignity comes in the attribution to man of the image and likeness of God. This is the creation of the total man, not just physical man, but surely the body is not excluded from this total dignity. Any system of values, such as Plato's, which devaluates the body and elevates the soul, is excluded. The total man is in the image of God — which does not, however, imply a "plastic"[1] concept of the image of God. All that needs to be said at this point is that the body is the worthy bearer of the image.

The account of man's creation in Genesis 2 does make these special points about the human body: it originates in the dust of the earth, it is formed by God, and the special spiration

1 Cf. J. K. Stamm, *Das Gottesebenbild des Menschen im Alten Testament* (*Theologische Studien*, Heft 54), p. 9.

of God makes it a living being. The spiration of God is not to be interpreted as a breathing of a soul into man (as in Roman Catholic exegesis of Gen. 2:7) but as that which makes man an animate being. On this score Jacob writes:

> The text then clearly affirms that the *nephesh* is not given to man as a soul which might be considered as deposited in a body but as the final result of divine activity which is a reality at once physical and spiritual; so that the most adequate translation of *nephesh chayyah* is 'living being.'[2]

Man is not a soul inhabiting a body; rather, by virtue of the divine spiration, he is an ensouled body.

A further indication of the dignity of the human body in the creation account is the pronouncement by the Creator that all things are good, i.e., they fulfill their divine intentionality (*telos*). Since man with his body is included under this pronouncement, he is of course also good.

Again, the pronouncement of a death penalty in Genesis 2 implies an estimate of the human body (2:17, also 3:19). M. E. Dahl makes it clear that death is not, in the scholastic sense, a mere separation of body and soul but a judgment upon the entire man.[3] Nevertheless the judgment includes the body, and comes to its most painful reminder in the death of the body. In its most comprehensive sense and in its direct physiological sense, death is the wages of sin. As Dahl also indicates, with the entrance of sin and death the *upward* direction and potential of man is reversed and now his existence has a *downward* slope toward the Void.[4] While some writers have maintained that according to the Scriptural view man is naturally mortal, nevertheless the way death is treated in Scripture seems to go contrary to this view. The Old

2 *Theology of the Old Testament*, p. 159. Cf.: "That man was shaped by God 'out of the dust of the ground,' and life breathed into him, is a basic affirmation of Hebrew "materialism." Man is *not* a noble spirit temporarily entombed in the evil matter of the body; he is not a double creature of body or matter and soul or spirit; but in his primal state he is a natural, unified creation having life in the same way as all God's living creatures" (R. G. Smith, "Dust," *A Theological Word Book of the Bible*, p. 70) .

3 *The Resurrection of the Body*, p. 53n.

4 *Ibid.*, p. 69.

Testament faith was that "man was not made for death, but that death came by sin . . . . Hence death is commonly conceived of as complete and utter isolation from God."[5]

The very fact that death is the acme of the divine judgment shows the importance of the body. The penalty must come to rest upon that which is equal to the seriousness of the fault. Unless the body were equal to this seriousness it would never be the locus of the wages of sin. This does not mean that the decease of the body exhausts the biblical notion of death, but it is central to it.

Another insight into the value of the body in Hebrew thought is seen in the physiological psychology of the Old Testament. There is almost a touch of behaviorism here. Psychical functions are attributed to the liver, the bones and kidneys. Further, it is interesting to note that whereas there are several words for the different parts of the human body there is no Hebrew word for the body as such.[6] The word body really indicates the total person.[7] A bit of Hebrewism crops up in English in such expressions as "anybody," "nobody," and "there wasn't a body to talk to."

In the New Testament we have the same general emphasis on the importance and worthiness of the body. The materials are extensive and have been reviewed for us in J. A. T. Robinson, *The Body, A Study in Pauline Theology*. Robinson is so bold as to write that "one could say without exaggeration that the concept of body forms the keystone of Paul's theology."[8]

In a summary way, the dignity of the body from the perspective of the New Testament can be stated as follows: (i) The Eternal Logos took flesh (John 1:14). Although "flesh" here means total human nature it includes the body. Unless

5 H. H. Rowley, *The Rediscovery of the Old Testament*, p. 223. Cullmann writes: "The belief in the resurrection presupposes the Jewish connection between death and sin." *Immortality of the Soul or Resurrection from the Dead*, p. 28.

6 J. A. T. Robinson, *The Body, A Study in Pauline Theology*, lists all the Old Testament words for body (p. 11n.).

7 "Man is a psycho-physical being and psychical functions are bound so closely to his physical nature that they are all localized in bodily organs which themselves only draw their life from the vital force which animates them." Jacob, *op. cit.*, p. 157.

8 *Op. cit.*, p. 9.

the human body were worthy of the dignity of the incarnation there never would have been an incarnation. (ii) The Saviour suffered for our sins by bearing them in his body on the tree (I Pet. 2:24). Here again it would be unwise to say he suffered in his body but not in his soul, but it is true that the sufferings of his body were part of the redemptive sufferings of Christ. Thus part of the weight of world redemption was born by this body, and this could not be unless the body were worthy of such a function. (iii) Paul uses the head and the body as an analogy of Christ's relationship to his Church (Eph. 3:6, 4:4, 12-16). Unless the body were held in proper worth by Paul he would never allow such an analogy to stand, whether he drew it himself or derived it from other sources. (iv) Finally, Paul states that the human body is the shrine of the Holy Spirit and therefore we can glorify God in our bodies (I Cor. 6:19-20). Here again unless the body were held in the highest regard it could never be the temple of the Spirit or an organ whereby we glorify God.

There is a passage by Eckermann on the body of Goethe that conveys in a remarkable way the sense of regard for the body that we find in both the Old and New Testaments. Eckermann (Goethe's "Boswell") writes as follows:

> The morning after Goethe's death, a deep desire seized me to look once again upon his earthly garment. His faithful servant, Frederick, opened for me the chamber in which he was laid out. Stretched upon his back, he reposed as if asleep; profound peace and security reigned in the features of his sublimely noble countenance. The mighty brow seemed yet to harbour thoughts. I wished for a lock of his hair; but reverence prevented me from cutting it off. The body lay naked, only wrapped in a white sheet; large pieces of ice had been placed near it, to keep it fresh as long as possible. Frederick drew aside the sheet, and I was astonished at the divine magnificence of the limbs. The breast was powerful, broad, and arched; the arms and thighs were full, and softly muscular; the feet were elegant, and of the most perfect shape; nowhere, on the whole body, was there a trace either of fat or of leanness and decay. A perfect man lay in great beauty before me; and the rapture of the sight caused me to forget for a moment that the immortal spirit had left such an abode. I laid my hand on his heart — there

was a deep silence — and I turned away to give free vent to my
suppressed tears.[9]

We thus come to an important conclusion. According to
both the Old and New Testaments the body is an integral,
dignified part of the total self. The human person is a unity
and a totality of the material and the spiritual. Consequently
the strict dualisms of Plato, Descartes, and religious liberalism
are unbiblical. The latter went astray in looking at the
human body almost as a hangover from man's brute ancestry
and therefore deplored any doctrine of the resurrection as
gross materialism.

The insights of A. E. Taylor are surprising and unexpected
at this point. He accuses the Platonic doctrine of immortality
(and with it that of religious liberalism) of teaching the
survival of half a personality;[10] and he notes that a destiny for
man must be the destiny of *the whole man*.[11] In the biblical
doctrine of the whole man — including the body — we find
the foundations for a doctrine of the resurrection.

SECTION 28:   *The bodily resurrection of Christ*[12]

The resurrection of Christ from the dead is in harmony with
the Old and New Testament teaching that the whole man is
the body-soul man. Any other man is part man. On this
score Cullmann has written:

> The New Testament certainly knows the difference between
> body and soul, or more precisely, between the inner and the
> outer man. This distinction does not, however, imply oppo-
> sition, as if the one were by nature good, the other by nature
> bad. Both belong together, both are created by God. The
> inner man without the outer has no proper, full existence. It
> requires a body. It can, to be sure, somehow lead a shady ex-

9 *Conversations of Goethe with Eckermann (Everyman's Library)*, p.
426.
10 *The Christian Hope of Immortality*, p. 12.
11 *Ibid.*, p. 11.
12 Cf. Eduard Lohse, *Die Auferstehung Jesu Christi im Zeugnis des
Lukasevangeliums*. Karl Barth, *Auslegung von Matthäus 28, 16-20*. Gerhard
Koch, *Die Auferstehung Jesu Christi*. H. D. A. Major, "The Resurrection
of Jesus Christ, *The Mission and Message of Jesus*, pp. 211-218.

istence without the body, like the dead in Sheol according to the Old Testament, but that is not a *genuine life*.[13]

If the resurrection is to the fullness of life it must be the resurrection of the total man. Therefore the resurrection is *bodily*. It is true that man may exist as spirit (Heb. 12:23) but to be without a heavenly body is to be naked (II Cor. 5:3), something which the apostle feared. Consequently our Redeemer, after suffering for our sins and being buried, rose bodily from the dead on the third day.

It is true that the four Gospel accounts vary widely[14] and attempts at ready harmonization are difficult. It is also true that our ignorance of risen bodies is far greater than our information and therefore we should be guided by a holy restraint.[15] Nevertheless the reports are clear enough that in some genuine sense the resurrection of Christ was bodily. We gather from the reports that the following may be said of the bodily character of the resurrection of Christ.

(i) He rose from the dead in a substantial body. Our Lord clearly stated that he was not a spirit but invited his disciples to see his hands and feet and recognize that he had flesh and bones (Luke 24:39). To put the question beyond all doubt he asked for broiled fish and ate it (v. 43).[16] The women were able to grasp his feet (Matt. 28:9, John 20:17). He had hands that he could lift up (Luke 24:50). He could breathe upon the disciples (John 20:22). Thomas was invited to put his finger in the marks of crucifixion and place his hand in the riven side of Christ (John 20:27).

Much is made in the Gospel record of the empty place exactly

13 *Immortality of the Soul or Resurrection from the Dead?* p. 33. Italics are his.

14 Major, *op. cit.*, gives a synoptic account of the details of the reports of the resurrection.

15 Major (*op. cit.*) lists the three possibilities of the character of the risen body: (1) That the crucified body was raised up; (2) that it was the same body spiritualized; (3) that it was an entirely different body, but since personalities that have gone on into the next world can only be known "bodily," he manifested himself in a bodily manner.

16 Commenting on Luke 24:39 Lohse says: "No, the manifestation of the Lord was no ghostly manifestation, but the Risen One convinced the disciples that he had risen bodily." *Op. cit.*, p. 35.

where the Lord was put to rest. His body was missing even though the grave clothes remained! In this connection Koch writes that "the empty tomb with its emphasis on the bodiliness of the Risen One erects an immovable barrier against any spiritualizing of the event."[17]   And in harmony with this Barth writes that the reports "speak of real events in space and time, not of some sort of thoughts and ideas. They speak of an empty grave . . . of the body of the person of Jesus which was visible, hearable, and touchable."[18]

Besides the empty tomb, the bodily character of the resurrection is emphasized by the nearness of the appearances of Christ to the tomb and to the city of his crucifixion, but most important of all, by its happening on the third day. Lohse correctly notes that the third day was not specified in order to show that the resurrection fulfilled some Old Testament prophecy, but rather to indicate a fixed datum! Continuing, Lohse comments that although usual methods of proving and testing do not apply here, nevertheless the intent of the reports is to make clear that: (1) God did something in history; (2) he did it at a certain place, Jerusalem; (3) he did a certain thing, he raised Christ from the dead; and (4) he did it at a certain time, the third day.[19]

Accordingly Christ is called the first-born from the dead (Col. 1:18, Rev. 1:5). This means that he is the first risen of a new humanity that shall share with him in the glory of a risen body.

(ii) The body of Christ was of the new order, the eschatological order, the order of the new age. As Koch says, "the resurrection of Jesus is God's deed of resurrection and is as such the inbreaking of the eschaton."[20]   The movement is, as Koch further notes, not a raising of Christ to super-history or super-temporality but rather the breaking of the eschaton into history.[21]   This is further emphasized by the fact that the entire initiative in the resurrection appearances is taken by

17 Op. cit., p. 166.
18 Op. cit., p. 6.
19 Op. cit., p. 17.
20 Op. cit., p. 55.
21 Ibid., p. 56.

the Risen One. In his own right and sovereignty as the risen Lord, he chooses where and when he shall make himself known.

The unique character of the resurrection records is to be found in the manner in which Christ shows his continuity with his life before his death and burial, and yet the discontinuity. *The Risen One is none other than the Crucified One!* He arose from the grave in which he was buried; he exhibits his wounds to show the continuity of his risen body with his crucified body and he partakes of food as a reminder of the Last Supper. Yet there is discontinuity. He can appear and disappear! He can pass through grave clothes without disturbing them. He can ascend in a cloud.

This continuity-discontinuity is seen in the kind of history here reported. It is *eventful* history. Christ appears as his own witness and imparts a compelling witness to his disciples. Paul gives a list of such appearance (I Cor. 15:5-8).[22] Yet it is the doings of the Risen One which are quite outside the reaches of ordinary historiography.[23]

It was Calvin's suggestion that the life of the body of the risen Lord was the life of the Holy Spirit.[24] Hence the Risen One is no longer in need of ordinary means of sustenance. His body is already the body of the new heavens, the new earth, the new Jerusalem.[25] He has already entered into the end-time

22 It is generally recognized that I Cor. 15:1ff. is very primitive Christianity. It is Paul's self-witness to the "official list" of the Church. It therefore must date as early as Paul's own conversion, which is now generally held to be about three years after the resurrection of Christ. The women are not included in the appearances of Christ, as this would not constitute evidence to the Jewish mind. The verb ōphthē used by Paul is also used in the Old Testament for the appearances of God.

23 Lohse points out that these events of the appearing of Christ were to make the apostles witnesses. It was not a series of neutral events which could be observed without faith and obedience. But it was Christ's self-witnessing which drew the apostles into the role of witnesses; and since these appearances are part of the foundations of the gospel they can be responded to only by faith and not so-called "historical faith." Cf. *op. cit.,* pp. 13-14.

24 So Cullmann too. *Op. cit.,* p. 37.

25 Barth takes the forty-day appearance as the fulfillment of Christ's words that some would see him in his kingdom of power and glory. *Op. cit.,* pp. 5f. For this reason some theologians take the resurrection and the second coming as part of the same event.

in his resurrection, for the end-time powers were revealed in his resurrection.

(iii) It was a glorious body. Paul calls it a glorious body (Phil. 3:21). Certainly the attributes of the risen body of believers described by Paul in I Corinthians 15:42-44 apply to the body of Christ. One of these attributes is glory. Although our Lord did veil the full radiance of his body, so that he could be mistaken for a gardner by Mary or be accepted merely as a stranger by the disciples on the road to Emmaus, yet he could also manifest his glory. Stephen saw the glory of God and Christ standing at his right hand (Acts 7:55). When Christ appeared to Paul it was in a glory that was more dazzling than the noonday sun (Acts 9:3, 22:6, 26:13).

The important matter, however, is not the radiance of the body as such. It is stated in the book of Revelation that the light of the New Jerusalem is the glory of God, and the lamp is the Lamb of God (Rev. 22:23). What is important is that the body of Christ, whatever its composition, is a body of glory.

(iv) There is a relationship between the resurrection of Christ and the resurrection of believers. Paul claims that believers shall have a glorious body like Christ's (Phil. 3:21). It has already been noted that Christ as the first begotten from the dead is the Head of a new humanity risen from the dead. In I Corinthians 15:45 Christ is called *a life-giving spirit*. All who are spiritually joined to Christ, who are in Christ, shall thus share in the resurrection of Christ at his appearing. Paul speaks of orders (*tagma*) of the resurrection. First Christ the first fruits (*aparxē*), then those who are his at his coming (I Cor. 15:23-24). The latter, we must conclude, will enter into the glory of Christ's risen body and share this glory in their own bodies.

SECTION 29: *The glorification of the believer in his bodily resurrection*

Paul speaks of the sufferings that are now and the glory that shall be (Rom. 8:18). Part of the glory that shall be is the redemption of the body, by which Paul means its resurrection (v. 23). This is the hope in which we are saved, and

while not enjoying its reality we await it with patience (v. 25).
Indeed, as Paul says in I Corinthians 15:12-19, without this
hope the Christian life is meaningless.

Regin Prenter has expressed himself strongly on this point,
insisting that if this hope dies out of the Church then all
meaning is drained from the Christian faith.[26] Prenter adds
that the resurrection of the body is not an appendage to our
faith, which could be excised without any loss. Rather, it
is of such vital importance that its loss is the loss of everything.

Some years ago Fosdick[27] wrote that he believed in the
persistence of personality through death but not in the resurrection of the flesh. Since we have now achieved a "rarefied
conception of the soul" we are no longer bound to "the old
category" of the resurrection of the body. But recent studies
in biblical theology are very much contrary to Fosdick. The
reason has already been stated, namely, that man is the total
man. Therefore any considerations of the future life must
be about the total man and not half a man. M. E. Dahl
discusses "The Semitic Totality Concept" at some length,
showing the totality of the biblical view of man.[28] The inclusion
of the body in the plan of redemption and the focussing of the
Christian hope on the resurrection of the body are therefore
deeply rooted in the biblical doctrine of man.

The New Testament evidence is clear that the resurrection
of our bodies is part of our glorification. There are three
passages in particular that are important for this consideration.

(i) Philippians 3:21. This passage teaches that God shall
transform (literally, "change the schema of") our bodies
which are now bodies of humiliation into bodies like (sum-

---

26 *Schöpfung und Erlösung*, pp. 541-544. Thus any evaporation of the
Christian hope into a mere doctrine of immortality is also the evaporation of
Christianity. In a beautiful passage speaking of the freedom into which
God calls us by his electing grace, Barth speaks of our being "free from
the bondage in which the curse works itself out, free from death." *Church
Dogmatics*, II/2, p. 30.

27 *The Modern Use of the Bible*, pp. 98-101.

28 *The Resurrection of the Dead*, Chapter 5. Cf. also E. C. Rust, *Nature and Man in Biblical Thought*. D. R. G. Owen, *Body and Soul*. F. J.
Taylor, "Body," *Theological Word Book of the Bible*. Oscar Cullmann,
op. cit. Dahl, *op. cit.* J. A. T. Robinson, *The Body* (and extensive literature cited).

morphos) the glorious body of Christ. The word *summorphos* strongly emphasizes the likeness, the similarity between Christ's body and our body. The body of Christ is specified as a body of glory, and our bodies shall be changed into bodies like his.

Then Paul adds that God is able to do this "by the power which enables him even to subject all things to himself." This is the New Testament answer to all technical objections to the resurrection (e.g., cremation, or a body lost in the sea and consumed by thousands of minute organisms). As Dahl indicates, the New Testament writers were not concerned with "particles."[29] They knew the whole body. No atomic theory or cellular theory was in their minds. Loosing himself from physical and metaphysical speculation, Paul attributes the resurrection of the body *to the divine power which is God's ability to subject everything to himself.* There can be no technical difficulty with a God of this power. If he can subject everything to himself he can certainly overcome the technical problems of the resurrection.

(ii) II Corinthians 5:1-5. In this passage Paul contrasts our present earthly (and earthy) *tent* with our future heavenly *building.* This building is not made with hands but is eternal in the heavens. While living in this tent we groan, wanting to live in a building, and so not be found naked.[30] Paul does not yearn for the naked state but he wants to be clothed with immortality in order that "what is mortal may be swallowed up by life" (v. 4). This is a remarkably strong expression. The "mortal" is certainly the mortal body. It is to be so clothed with immortality that mortality will be "gulped down" (*katapinō*) into extinction. One could hardly express more strongly a denial of a doctrine of mere immortality of the soul or more emphatically the immortality of the body.

Again in this passage Paul deals with the "technical" problem. The Christian has now, in this life, the Holy Spirit as his guarantee (v. 5). God has made this preparation for

---

29 *Op. cit.,* p. 47.

30 Two interpretations of "naked" are possible. (i) It may refer to the state of the souls of Christians dead in Christ; (ii) it may refer to being found at the last day without a heavenly building. Oepke prefers the second. *TWNT,* I, 774

the events ahead. In his time the eschatological powers of the Holy Spirit will be released and our mortality will be "gulped down" with immortality! It is the Spirit that shall clothe our nakedness with an eternal, heavenly building.

(iii) I Corinthians 15:38-50.[31] Speaking of the resurrection body Paul says of man that God shall give him a body (v. 38). This again is the "technical" problem answered. Not in any theory of corpuscles or cells or particles or natural theology, but directly in the act of God himself is found the answer to the resurrection of the body. To describe this body Paul sets up a series of four duads in which he contrasts our present body with the body that shall be.

Our present bodies are perishable, capable of disease and death (*phthora*). The resurrection body is incorruptible, immortal and immune to all powers of decay and destruction (*aphtharsia*).

Our present bodies are bodies that are dishonored, disgraced, and humiliated (*atimia*). The resurrection body is a body of glory, of supreme divine approval (*doxa*).

Our present bodies are bodies of moral and spiritual weakness unable to respond to the divine will (*asthenia*). The resurrection body is able perfectly to respond to the divine will, for it is characterized by power (*dunamis*).

Our present bodies are made for life on this planet under present conditions (*psuchikon*). Our risen bodies are eschatological bodies, enlivened by the Holy Spirit (*pneumatikon*), and thus fitted for the New Jerusalem.

In short, the four positive attributes of the resurrection body may be equated with the glorification of that body. This glorification is no process, no matter of growth, but occurs suddenly, dramatically, at the end-time (I Cor. 15:52).

---

31 Dahl, *op. cit.*, gives a summary of the leading interpretations of the entire fifteenth chapter with his own new attempt.

VII The Glorification and the New Jerusalem

SECTION 30: *The relationship of man to creation*

The Scriptures commence the creation-account with the creation of the heavens and the earth, its sea, plant, and animal populations, and conclude it with the creation of man, who is made its lord. They present us with a cosmos related to man and not a cosmos in itself.[1] There is, then, a close bond between man and creation. This is a theme which runs throughout all of Scripture and comes to particular focus in relationship to Israel and her land.[2]

Man is not beyond creation even though he is its lord (Gen. 1:28). Like the animals he is made from common dust (Gen. 2:7). Therefore he exists within the cosmos as part of it and sustains *a dynamic-spiritual* relationship to the cosmos.

Equally impressive in Scripture is the unity and harmony of soul and body in man. Man is a totality, a living being. What happens to the inner man cannot be severed from the outer man, whether this be his body, his culture, or his cosmos. Unless we understand this vital nexus we cannot understand man in creation or man in sin.

The Edenic picture is a picture of harmony. Man is in harmony with himself. He is in harmony with woman, his helpmeet. He is in harmony with his cosmos as it manifests itself in the garden.

1 Cf. Karl Barth, *Church Dogmatics*, III/2, pp. 3-19, where Barth makes it clear why there is in Scripture a man-related cosmology and not a world-view cosmology.
2 Cf. E. C. Rust, *Nature and Man in Biblical Thought*, for an exceptionally thorough study of the nexuses of relationship between God and man, God and nature, man and nature, and Israel and the land.

When sin enters, all these fundamental harmonies are altered. The disobedience of the inner man leads to a judgment upon the outer man. Woman will now suffer pain of childbirth. Man will now return to dust. But something happens to the cosmos as well. It becomes cursed: the pestilence of weeds is promised, and man can earn his bread only by the sweat of his brow. Something also happens to society. There is fratricide (Cain and Abel), a degenerate civilization destroyed by the flood, and a rebellious society dispersed at the tower of Babel.

Just as sin represents the disturbance of the harmonies of man, redemption calls for the restoration of these harmonies. But this restoration is according to order. First comes the restoration of the inner man by regeneration and justification. At the return of Christ the outer man is restored by the resurrection from the dead. But the Scriptures do not stop here. There must be a healing of the cosmos. Consequently new heavens and a new earth are promised. But there must also be the healing of society, and this takes the form of the New Jerusalem. That there is this nexus of body-soul-cosmos is taught in Romans 8:18-25, a passage we shall examine in some detail later.

SECTION 31: *The glorification of the Christian and the renewal of creation*

Coincident with the great messianic passages of the latter part of Isaiah is the promise of a new heaven and a new earth.[3] This promise is taken up and repeated in the New Testament and forms part of the pattern of glorification. It is in keeping with the thesis developed in Section 30 that man and the cosmos are dynamically related, and if man is to be glorified the cosmos is to be renewed. Important New Testament passages dealing with this theme are the following:

(i) Matthew 19:28. This passage speaks of the Son of Man on his glorious throne in the new world, the *paliggenesia*.

---

3 Cf. *"The Renovation of Nature,"* Sanday and Headlam, *Romans, ICC,* pp. 210-212. G. Vos, "New Heavens and New Earth," *ISBE,* II, 1353-1354.

The word *paliggenesia* means a restoration, a renewal.[4] It
is paralleled in Luke 22:30 by "my kingdom" and in Mark
10:30 by "in the age to come." Büchsel says that wrapped up
in this word is the Jewish faith in the resurrection of the dead
and world renewal.[5] Thus the *paliggenesia* is the cosmic re-
ordering of all things and coincides with the manifestation of
the Messiah in his glory.

(ii) II Peter 3:1-13. Peter says that all things do not
continue from the creation in unbroken succession. The flood
was a great natural disturbance which came as a judgment of
God. The present heavens and earth shall not continue forever, for they, too, await an hour of judgment, this time of
fire and not of water. But this is not the end of things, for
"according to his promise we wait for new heavens and a
new earth in which righteousness dwells" (*katoikeō*, to take up
permanent residence.) The promise mentioned by Peter can
only mean the promises of the Old Testament, for he also
uses the rich Old Testament expression, "the day of the Lord"
(v. 10).

(iii) Revelation 21:1. In this verse John writes that he
saw a new heaven and a new earth, for the first heavens
and earth had passed away. As Strack-Billerbeck shows,[6]
world-renewal was a great rabbinic theme. And coincident
with the great dramatic conclusion of world history recorded
in the latter chapters of the book of Revelation is the new
heaven and the new earth as the cosmic renewal necessary
for the New Jerusalem. The word *new* is itself an eschatological word.[7] The culmination of redemption is to bring
into existence the new, so that the theme of eschatology
could well be that given in Revelation 21:5, "Behold, I make
all things new."[8]

4 Dalman says that it is an unusual expression which cannot be translated back into Hebrew or Aramaic so must be the expression of the
author. *The Words of Jesus*, p. 177.

5 *TWNT*, I, 687.

6 *Kommentar*, III, 840f.

7 Behm, *TWNT*, III, 451.

8 The new has already begun. Salvation is called a new creation.
With *neos* we have the new wine (Matt. 9:17); the new dough (I Cor.
5:7); the new man (Col. 3:10); and a new covenant (Heb. 12:24). With

(iv) Romans 8:17-26. This is the most important of the passages which deal with the renewing of the cosmos. Paul speaks of suffering with Christ as the precondition of being glorified with Christ (v. 17). In enlarging on the contrast between present sufferings and future glory he sketches out the whole doctrine of the correlation of our redemption with the renewal of the creation.

Paul says that the creation was subjected by a divine sentence (*hupetagē*) to futility (*mataiotēs*).[9] But this judgment of futility is solely the fault of man. Because man sinned, creation cannot fulfill its original *telos*, which was to be man's wonderful habitat.[10] Many effects of this judgment can now be seen. Death, which Paul calls a bondage to decay (v. 21), is its most universal sign. In general, the creation groans and travails. What is exactly meant here by "creation" is not easy to determine, but we must remember that biblical cosmology is man-related cosmology and therefore the best commentary on this matter is Genesis 3.

Even the Christian does not escape this judgment, for he, too, groans inwardly (v. 23) as he must endure all the problems of bodily existence under the bondage to decay. He, too, experiences the *pathēmata* (v. 18) of the present age. These *pathēmata* must be taken in the total sense as referring to all the forms of frustration and suffering under which we must live in the present age.[11] Finally, we are, as Christians, beset with such spiritual weakness (v. 26) that we need a special ministry of the Holy Spirit to enable even our prayers to be offered properly.

The present depressing conditions of suffering, bondage, and weakness will end at the glorification of the believer. This is not something we can guess from the nature of things

---

kainos and *kainotēs* we have the new covenant; the new teaching (Mark 1:27); the new commandment (John 13:34); the new creation (II Cor. 5:17); the new man (Eph. 2:5); the new life (Rom. 6:4); and the newness of the Spirit (Rom. 7:6).

9 Bauernfeind observes that this futility is bracketed at its beginning and at its end by God. *TWNT*, IV, 529.

10 Sanday and Headlam say that the opposite to futility is *teleios*, perfection. When something is subjected to *mataiotēs* it cannot reach its *teleios. Op. cit.*, p. 208.

11 *TWNT*, V, 933.

but comes as a revelation (v. 19). We shall be glorified with Christ as his fellow heirs (v. 18). This coming glory contrasts radically with our present sufferings, in fact so much so that our present sufferings are to be counted as nothing (cf. II Cor. 4:17, "For this slight momentary afflication is preparing us for an eternal weight of glory beyond all comparison").

In the glorification of the Christian comes the renewal of the cosmos and so the heartfelt longing of the cosmos (*apokaradokia*) is for the glorification of the sons of God.[12] The creation knows that it is in bondage until this happens. But when this takes place the corruption to bondage will be lifted and the creation will be set free and so obtain the glorious liberty of the children of God (v. 21). Thus the significant mark of this glorification for both creation and the human body is *freedom*. It is freedom from frustration, corruption, suffering, and weakness. It is freedom for the original *telos* of God. Hence freedom (as already noted) takes its place as one of the great words of eschatology and glorification.

In these passages of Scripture we have seen that part of the process of glorification is the glorification of the cosmos. According to some writers it is called a world-renewal, according to others the making of new heavens and a new earth, and according to Paul setting free from bondage into the glorious liberty of the children of God.

SECTION 32: *The New Jerusalem*

The first habitat of man was a garden, but his final habitat is a city. It is interesting to ask, Why *does* man spend his eternal life in a city and not in a garden or a country (i.e., a New Palestine)? The question is all the more pertinent when it is realized that the Jews never developed the notion of a

---

12 "A man is therefore a man only as he possesses 'a world.' The non-human cosmos is no indifferent appendage of man's existence. It signifies that the good God gives to us enduring space for human existence [*Lebensraum*]. Therefore the hope and the resurrection is also a hope for the regeneration of the world." R. Prenter, *Schöpfung und Erlösung*, p. 543.

city-state.[13] Jerusalem was made the capital city of the Hebrew nation by David and thereby became one of the great cities of the ancient world. It was not only the capital where the king was, and where the military power was centered, but because the Temple was built there it was also the religious center of the land and of the people. Hence it receives such honorific titles as the city of God, the city of the great king, and the holy city.

Next, the city became identified with the religious life of the people. The fate of Jerusalem was the fate of the people. The city became idealized and symbolized and so stood for the hopes and aspirations of the people. This is so poignantly expressed in Psalm 137:5-6, "If I forget you, O Jerusalem, let my right hand wither! Let my tongue cleave to the roof of my mouth, if I do not remember you, if I do not set Jerusalem above my highest joy!" Such thoughts about Jerusalem as the symbol of the hopes of Israel were nourished, developed, and expanded during the inter-biblical period.[14]

But the New Testament does not pursue this idealization of the earthly Jerusalem. In fact, it takes a sharply critical attitude towards it and looks forward to its destruction. The hope is transferred from the renovation of the earthly Jerusalem (which was a theme of the inter-biblical period) to a *new* Jerusalem. Thus the main lines can be traced from the garden to the ancient fortress of Jerusalem to the city of Jerusalem to its idealization in the Psalms to the renovated Jerusalem of the inter-biblical period to the New Jerusalem of the New Testament. De Young devotes an entire chapter to the theme of "The Rejection of Jerusalem" (Chapter III) in which he shows that the idealization and renovation of the earthly city was rejected by the writers of the New Testament and their hope turned to the New, the Eschatological Jerusalem which shall come down out of heaven from God. For example, he writes:

13 Cf. the comprehensive article by Strathmann on *"polis," TWNT*, VI, 516-536, especially p. 529. Cf. also the monograph by J. C. De Young, *Jerusalem in the New Testament*.

14 Cf. Strathmann, *op. cit.*, and *Dictionary of the Apostolic Church*, II, 85-86, where many excerpts from the literature are cited.

Jerusalem has lost all redemptive significance for the Christian because Christ has made the final sacrifice for sin outside the gates of Jerusalem, and redemption can only be found where he is — without the camp. Jerusalem has lost all eschatological significance; there is no abiding city on earth; hence the Christian, like Abraham, looks for the city which is to come . . . the city of the living God, the heavenly Jerusalem . . . whose builder and maker is none other than God himself . . . . Thus the eschatological hope of Judaism is radically different from that of Christianity. The emphasis in the eschatology of the N. T. as well as that of early Christianity is not on the earthly city. On the contrary, as far as the Christian faith is concerned, the redemptive significance of Jerusalem and the temple came to an abrupt end with the death of Christ. The faith and expectation of the Christian is directed away from the earthly city to the heavenly and the new Jerusalem.[15]

The concept of the New Jerusalem corresponds to the concept of the new heavens and the new earth. Man's soul, his body, his environment and his cosmos form one nexus. Redemption is not final until it has worked its effect in the entire nexus. If man's redeemed soul calls for a redeemed body, the redeemed body calls for a redeemed environment. Thus the Scriptural revelation concludes when the book of Revelation portrays a new cosmos and a New Jerusalem. It is within this glorified city that the glorified saints will exist eternally. According to direct statement and by implication the New Jerusalem must be drawn into the structure of glorification. That it is implied in view of the body-soul-environment nexus we have already argued. It is also a matter of direct statement, however, for the New Jerusalem is spoken of as having "the glory of God" (Rev. 21:11) .

It has already been mentioned that the New Testament passes from the notion of a revived or renovated *earthly* Jerusalem to a heavenly Jerusalem. Even so, some traces of the Old Testament regard for Jerusalem carry over into the New Testament. In Matthew 4:5 it is called the holy city, and in Matthew 5:35 Jesus calls it the city of the great king. Nevertheless Jesus himself spoke of the desolation of the earthly Jerusalem and

15 *Op. cit.,* pp. 109, 116. Chapter IV is entitled, "The Eschatological Jerusalem."

therefore the end of any hope in terms of the glorification of the earthly Jerusalem.[16]

In Hebrews the men of faith expect a city (*polis*, Heb. 11:10), a fatherland (*patria*, 11:14), and a kingdom (*basileia*, 12:28). These terms are virtually synonymous and express that hope which finds its culmination in the New Jerusalem. But it is interesting to see how this inheritance is qualified. Abraham looked for a city which had foundations (*themelios*, Heb. 11:10). He had left a city with foundations and went to live in tents (v. 9) but he was looking for a city which had foundations laid by God.[17] God will not only lay the foundation but he is the architect (*technitēs*) and builder (*dēmiourgos*) of the city.

Looking back over the lives of the men of faith, the writer next says that these men were seeking a fatherland (*patria*) which was different from their own national homeland, for if they had been primarily interested in their national homeland they would have returned to it. But they are seeking a better fatherland, and this word "better" is one of the key-words of Hebrews, signifying the fulfillment and the reality of the true religion of Christianity in contrast to the religion of the Old Testament with its shadows and types. The *patria* which they seek is a better one than they left, for it is a heavenly (*epouranios*) one. "Heavenly" means, first, that the hope for the new fatherland is *superior* to the older Jewish hope, and that it is an *eschatological* hope.[18] And this heavenly fatherland is then identified with the city prepared by God. The Greek word "prepared" (*etoimazō*) is a very important one. It is a strong word for the divine action in creation, providence, and redemption.[19] The true fatherland of the pilgrim is the

16 Cf. De Young, *op. cit.*, "A. The teaching of Jesus [on the rejection of Jerusalem]," pp. 76ff.

17 As Schmidt points out, already in the Old Testament there is present the concept of a city built upon divinely laid foundations (Isa. 28:16). In a beautiful description of a restored Jerusalem we are told that its foundation will be of saphire (Isa. 54:11). *TWNT*, III, 64.

18 *TWNT*, V, 540-541.

19 Grundmann says that in this word the entire vivacity of the biblical concept of God pulses. *TWNT*, II, 702.

city which God in his power and in his redemptive will has prepared.

In Hebrews 12 the writer speaks of a kingdom which the Christians shall receive. The remarkable character of this kingdom is that it cannot be shaken (saleuō). All human kingdoms can be shaken, i.e., overturned, dislodged, conquered. The present order is the old order (eschatologically speaking) and God will shake it by bringing it to an end. But in the midst of the old order is already the new order, and it cannot be dislodged in the final shaking of all things. Consequently the author invites his readers to receive that eschatological kingdom which will survive the divine shaking. Thus we presume that the fatherland, the city, and the kingdom are one and that they find their eschatological end and glorious state in the new Jerusalem.

The final reference in Hebrews is in 12:22, "But you have come to Mount Zion and to the city of the living God, the heavenly Jerusalem." Obviously the three expressions are synonymous: Zion, the city of God, and the heavenly Jerusalem are the same entity.[20] The remarkable item here is the sharp break of the New Testament with the inter-biblical faith in a renovated Jerusalem. Here is no glorification of the ancient fortress of David but a displacement of it. And this Mount Zion, this city of the living God, this heavenly Jerusalem reaches its final destination and glory in the New Jerusalem of Revelation 21.

Somewhat similar to the treatment of Jerusalem in Hebrews is Paul's treatment in Galatians 4:21-31. Hagar, the law, the slave woman, the Old Covenant, Mt. Sinai, and the present Jerusalem form one complex. Concerning this passage De Young writes: "Gal. 4:21ff. represents, perhaps, the sharpest polemic against Jerusalem and Judaism in the N. T. It must have been quite a shock to the Jews to have their holy city linked up with Hagar and her seed."[21] The free woman, the promise, the Jerusalem that is above, our mother, form the second complex. This second Jerusalem is characterized by

20 De Young, op. cit., p. 141.
21 Ibid., p. 106.

two words: above (ano) and free (eleuthera).[22] Ano is not
here primarily spatial but refers to the spiritual superiority of
the heavenly Jerusalem over the city of Jerusalem.[23] The basic
meaning of freedom is freedom from sin in contrast to the
bondage of sin engendered by the law.[24] There is no overtone
of the eschatological Jerusalem possessing the glory of God
in this passage, but it is in harmony with the other revelation
of the New Jerusalem.

The New Jerusalem is the eternal home of the redeemed,
in which city the Triune God lives in unbroken communion
with the redeemed. The entire description of it is one of
glory. Glorified saints live in a glorious city in glorious existence
surrounded by the new cosmos.

Certain things are attributed to the New Jerusalem. It is
called a city. It might have been a land that was glorified,
but Jewish piety and the prophetic Scriptures made Jerusalem,
the city, the symbol of righteousness, hope, and future glory.
Those who shall live in that city have their names enrolled,
not unlike the registry of citizenship of a city-state. This city
is also called holy (Rev. 21:2). Here is a word with rich
Old and New Testament associations.[25] It combines here
both the notion of the sacred and the pure. It is sacred in
that it is the eternal city of God and it is pure in that nothing
unclean shall enter it. It is called a new city (Rev. 21:2).
It has already been noted that new is a great eschatological
word for both the entire New Testament and especially the
book of Revelation. It is the city which fulfills the promise;
it is the realized city; it is the final city; and it is the glorified
city. As De Young remarks, there is a world of difference
between the eschatological New Jerusalem and the idealized
city of Plato.[26]

Furthermore, it is the city which comes down from heaven
(Rev. 21:2). This speaks of its origin. It is not a city made
by man, like Babylon, nor an earthly Jerusalem "retooled" for

22 Ibid., p. 128.
23 TWNT, I, 377.
24 TWNT, II, 492.
25 "Hagios," TWNT, I, 116-123.
26 Op. cit., p. 120.

eternity. It is a city whose architect, contractor, and builder is God; it is therefore distinct from the glorified earthly Jerusalem for which the Jews hoped. It comes down to earth! Eternity is no Platonic existence in heaven but existence in a city on this earth. The story of man begins in a garden on this earth and ends in a city on the same earth (which has undergone its own glorification).

It is a beautiful city — *prepared as a bride for her husband* (Rev. 21:2). The verb in this phrase (*kosmeō*) is at the root of our English word "cosmetics." Basically it means to arrange, to set in order; then it means to array, to decorate. The New Jerusalem is not only holy but beautiful, fulfilling the goal of the tabernacle that it be beautiful and glorious. The details of the beautification of this city are given in the subsequent description.

The city is called the *dwelling of God* (Rev. 21:3), for God will dwell with them. The relationship between this statement and the tabernacle in the wilderness cannot be missed: "And let them make me a sanctuary, that I may dwell in their midst" (Exod. 25:8). To this must be added the great messianic-eschatological promise of Ezekiel: ". . . and will set my sanctuary in the midst of them for evermore. My dwelling place shall be with them; and I will be their God, and they shall be my people" (37:26-27). Thus the eternal Jerusalem is not only the eternal home of man but the city where God shall place his name eternally.

The specific characteristics of the New Jerusalem are spelled out in Revelation 21:11-22:5. John sees the city from a high mountain, which parallels very closely the experience of Ezekiel (40:2), who was set upon a high mountain over against the city of his vision. John sees it as a city "having the glory of God, its radiance like a most rare jewel, like a jaspar, clear as crystal" (Rev. 21:11).

The city is a glorified oriental city. It has huge walls, gates, and foundations. It is, architecturally, an idealized and schematized Jerusalem.

It is a city whose glory is represented through the use of expensive materials such as jewels and gold, and through the emphasis on transparency.

The structure is symbolic particularly in its numbering in

twelves or multiples thereof, the names of the twelve tribes, and the names of the twelve apostles.

The illumination of the city is the glory of God and the Lamb is the lamp thereof (Rev. 21:23, 22:5).

Such is the New Jerusalem, the eternal home of man and the eternal tabernacle of God. It is the glorified environment and glorified society which corresponds to the glorified soul and glorified body of the redeemed.

VIII   Glorification As Glorious Existence

SECTION 33:   *Glorious existence in the Pauline literature*

The process of glorification is not complete until the believer enters into a state of glorious existence within the New Jerusalem.   Many characteristics of this existence have already been discussed.   There are some other very suggestive passages, however, which illuminate the quality of this eternal glorious existence and still others that speak of it rather directly.

(i) It will be a glorious life in a prepared place and in perfect fellowship with Jesus Christ (John 14:2-3).   Our Lord uses a very general expression to speak of the eternal home of the Christian: "My Father's house."   In many Old Testament references and some New Testament references it means the temple, but here it means God's kingdom.[1]   Very close to this is John 8:35, "the slave does not continue in the house for ever; the son continues for ever."   This first verse speaks clearly of an eternal house (*oikia*) in which God's sons abide (*menō* — which is the verb form of the noun translated by rooms [*monai*] in the Revised Standard Version).   There is, then, an eternal abode, a homeland where God's sons abide forever.

This home has many rooms (*pollai monai*).   The dwelling of the Christian in God's house is in the many rooms within the house.   But these rooms are also called in the text "places" (*topoi*).   A *topos* can also mean a room, for it designates a place to live, to stay or to sit.   To prepare a place (*topos*) ahead of time is not too much unlike the modern practice of telegraphing for room reservations prior to arrival!

The place is prepared.   This verb "prepare" (*etoimadzō*)

1 Cf. *TWNT*, V, 125 and fn. 14.

is a customary eschatological one. It speaks of God's creative and preserving action for things present or future. Thus
it is a strong verb speaking of the great preparatory work of
Christ for our eternal dwelling with God. As Grundmann
suggests, it is the cross and the resurrection which truly prepare
a place for us.[2]

But we have not yet come to the essence of the passage. It
is a prepared place in our heavenly fatherland so that Jesus
Christ and his own — those who believe in him (John 14:1) —
might forever be together. The geographical proximity is but
the precondition for the eternal, blessed, glorious fellowship of
believers with their Saviour. This is blessed, heavenly existence!

(ii) It will be a glorious life in the eternal love of Christ
(Rom. 8:38-39). The great passage of Scripture about sin,
redemption, justification, and sanctification begins in Romans
1:16 and comes to its dramatic climax in Romans 8:37-38.
In the final analysis the greatest force maintaining Christians
in faith is the love of Christ. Therefore we are "super-con-
querers" (hypernikaō)!

Paul speaks not only of this life when he speaks of the
"love of God in Christ Jesus our Lord," but he speaks also
eschatologically. Death cannot separate us from this love
because it follows us through death. He also speaks of
"things to come": there is nothing in the future that can separate
us from this love. Therefore unto the end of time and into
eternity life in God's house shall be an existence within the
perfect love of Christ.

Ephesians 1:5 may possibly be appealed to here to sub-
stantiate this point. There is, however, a disagreement about
the location of the phrase "in love." Nevertheless, even if this
phrase be taken as applying to the initial phase of our redemption, we cannot deny that God's love follows us through to
the final phase of our redemption so that we shall be eternally
in the love of God in Christ.

(iii) It will be a glorious life in the fullness of knowledge
(I Cor. 13:10-13). In the midst of a discussion of gifts Paul
paints a marked contrast between our present knowledge and
our future knowledge. Part of our glorification is the bestowal

2 *TWNT*, II, 703.

upon the Christian of a perfection in knowledge. In discussing this theme Paul presents us with three contrasts:

Our present knowledge of God is that of a child (*nēpios*). We speak, we think, and we reflect as a child. But in glory our knowledge will be that of a man (*anēr*). Just as the man grows out of a childish way of speaking, thinking, and reflecting, and so turns and disowns his former childish ways, so in our knowledge of God in glory we shall utterly abandon our earthly kind of knowledge.[3]

Our present knowledge is a "prophetic knowledge." Kittel has made an extensive study of the word "mirror" (*esoptron*) and "enigma" (*ainigma*).[4] His opinion is that the expression does not mean that we see divine things in a turbid (*trüben*) mirror. According to his investigations the expression refers to prophetic knowledge, which by its nature is like a riddle. This prophetic knowledge gives way to face-to-face knowledge. This face-to-face knowledge is a perfect seeing of divine truth and a knowledge of true reality.[5] It is also important to note in this verse the contrast between now (*arti*) and then (*tote*). The "now" refers to the present life and its conditions and the knowledge which characterizes it, and the "then" refers to future, eschatological conditions and the knowledge that is possible under those conditions.

Our present knowledge is partial knowledge. We know God and his truth in a fragmentary way (*ek merous*).[6] But our knowledge in glory will be complete. As the divine mind knows us in fullness our human minds will then (again the contrast between *arti* and *tote*) know God and his truth with an analogical or parallel fullness.

(iv) It will be a glorious life in the fullness of the blessing of the kingdom of God. The kingdom of God is both present and future. In its future aspect it is as something the saints

---

3 Bertram observes that the child-man contrast is typical Hellenistic rhetoric. *TWNT*, IV, 920. Du Plessis notes that there is no gradual change of knowledge from that of a child to a man, but a radical change. *The Idea of Perfection in the New Testament*, p. 185. The verb is a strong one, *katargeō*, "to abolish." *TWNT*, I, 453.

4 *TWNT*, I, 177-179.

5 *TWNT*, VI, 778.

6 *TWNT*, IV, 600.

inherit (I Cor. 6:9, Eph. 5:5). In Ephesians 5:5 it is called "the kingdom of Christ and of God," showing the connection between Christ and the kingdom as well as the harmony between the Father and the Son.

This kingdom is a future, glorious kingdom, for God has called the believer to his kingdom and glory (I Thess. 2:12). Paul spoke of being saved for the heavenly kingdom (II Tim. 4:18). Putting these two verses together we catch the concept of a future, heavenly, glorious kingdom, which kingdom the saints in glory share.

The life in this glorious kingdom is suggested by three words in Romans 14:17. The kingdom of God is a kingdom in righteousness, peace, and joy.

The new heavens and earth are where righteousness takes up permanent residence (II Pet. 3:13). Righteousness is one of the greatest New Testament words, and it is not surprising to find it one of the characteristics of the city of God and the kingdom of God. It is a word with a strong forensic character,[7] but it is also a word of life. It is a word which not only states our glorious standing before God in perfect acceptance, but of the power of new life in Christ. Paul speaks strongly of the union of life and righteousness in Christian faith (Rom. 5:17, 21, 8:10). Thus the kingdom of God is characterized by righteousness as one of its most marked attributes. From this it follows that our glorified existence in the kingdom of God will be one in which our lives will be completely permeated by righteousness. If one may speak of the "totally depraved" sinner in this life one may well speak of the "totally righteous" person of the world to come.

The second great characteristic of the kingdom of God is peace.[8] Peace is just as remarkable a word as is righteousness. It is one of the great Old Testament words (*shalom*), meaning basically *wholeness* or *completeness*. Used of an individual it meant a healthy and good life, and used of the nation it meant

7 *TWNT*, II, 207.
8 *TWNT*, II, 398-418. E. M. Good, "Peace in the OT," *Interpreter's Dictionary of the Bible*, III, 704-706. C. L. Mitton, "Peace in the N.T.," *Interpreter's Dictionary of the Bible*, III, 706. C. F. Evans, "Peace," *A Theological Word Book of the Bible*, pp. 165-166.

prosperity and security. It is a word used frequently with reference to God, his blessings, his covenant and particularly of his salvation. Peace is one of the great blessings of the Messiah and his kingdom; in Isaiah this is presented in striking metaphors and pictures.

Peace is an equally impressive New Testament word. In John 14:27 our Lord said, "Peace I leave with you; my peace I give to you; not as the world gives do I give to you. Let not your hearts be troubled, neither let them be afraid." This is a most remarkable saying of our Lord. The messianic peace of the Old Testament is promised to his disciples. The realization of this peace is found in the redemption of Christ, for peace is set forth by Paul as one of the great accomplishments of Jesus Christ (Rom. 5:1, 8:6, 10:15, Eph. 2:14, 17, 6:15). Peace takes its place as part of Christian greetings, and God is called a God of peace. Therefore one of the attributes of the kingdom of God is peace, which Foerster calls the "eschatological salvation of the entire man."[9] Peace may then be defined *negatively* as the absence of all that disturbs and distresses, and *positively* as the presence of everything necessary for the completeness and wholeness of life. Therefore in our glorified state in the kingdom of God there shall be the complete absence of all that might disturb and distress and the complete presence of all that makes for the fullness and wholeness of life.

The third character of the kingdom of God is joy.[10] Like righteousness and peace, joy is at first one of the great words of Old Testament religion. In the Old Testament "religion is conceived of touching the deepest springs of emotion, including the feeling of exultant gladness which often finds outward expression in such actions as leaping, shouting and singing. Joy is repeatedly shown to be the natural outcome of fellowship with God."[11] Furthermore, like righteousness and peace, "joy" is a word rich with eschatological and messianic associations.

9 *TWNT,* II, 411.

10 Cf. D. Miall Edwards, "Joy," *ISBE,* III, 1755. Rudolph Bultmann, *Theology of the New Testament,* I, 339-340. D. Harvey, "Joy," *The Interpreter's Dictionary of the Bible,* II, 1000-1001. H. Gregor Smith, "Joy," *A Theological Word Book of the Bible,* p. 117.

11 Edwards. *op. cit.,* p. 1755.

Joy and rejoicing are prominent New Testament themes. Edwards sketches out how much joy there was in the earthly life of Christ. His depiction of his role as that of a bridegroom, his eating and drinking, his being charged with being a gluttonous man and winebibber, his rejoicing in the Holy Spirit, his attendance at social events, etc., all point to the joy in his life. There was certainly a deep-seated messianic joy. It was for joy that he suffered the cross (Heb. 12:2). Just as he asked that his messianic peace be given to his disciples, he asks that his messianic joy be given to them (John 15:11, 17:13).

The kingdom of God is then characterized by the fullness of a gladsome feeling based upon the realization of the messianic promises of Jesus Christ. The kingdom of God in its glorified state shall then be characterized by this joyous feeling in its most perfect and most full expression.

SECTION 34: *Glorious existence in the book of Revelation*

As can be expected from the nature of the case, the book of Revelation has some unusual passages concerning the glorious existence of the glorified saints. The first texts that shall be examined have to do with the conquerors among the seven churches of Revelation 2 and 3. Although these passages do not speak for all Christians they do give us an insight into the character of glorified existence, and for this reason they shall be examined.

(a) Revelation 2:7 says: "To him who conquers I will grant to eat of the tree of life, which is in the paradise of God." Part of the late Jewish hope expressed in apocalyptic and rabbinic literature was that the glorious age of the Messiah would be a restoration of Edenic (*Urzeit*) conditions. This was already suggested in such passages as Ezekiel 36:35 and Isaiah 51:3. Joined together were the renovated city of God, the tree of life, and the paradise of God. A paradise is a garden or park. The word is Persian in origin and was used by the translators of the Greek Septuagint for the garden of Eden. It was generally believed that the fruit of the tree of life would grant immortality to the eater.

In Revelation 2:7 the theme of the Jewish hope is picked up

and used, but as Jeremias notes, it undergoes a transformation.[12] *Jesus Christ is the Restorer of the lost paradise!* It was the Jewish hope that the Messiah would open the door of paradise, remove the sword which threatened Adam, and give the fruit of the tree of life to the saints. John boldly applies this role to Christ. Christ *gives* the right to the tree of life. This is a frequent expression in John's writings. It first of all signifies the privileges and functions of the Son, and secondly that which the Son bestows upon his followers.[13]

The paradise of God is the New Jerusalem,[14] which thus represents an environment of perfection created by the divine power. To eat of the tree of life means to enter into "all the possibilities of a complete and glorious life," for the one who overcomes is "prepared to become immortal in a vastly higher sense than was possible to primitive man."[15] Thus glorification is not only an entering into a perfected and glorious environment but it is also the full partaking of the fullness of life in that environment represented in our text by eating of the tree of life in the paradise of God.

(b) Revelation 2:10 says: "Be faithful unto death, and I will give you the crown of life." Crowns and diadems were an integral part of life in the New Testament world. Crowns were garlands or wreaths bestowed upon men for valor in battle, service in political life, and victory in games. The gods also were crowned beings. Some commentators think that the conquerer in this passage receives a garland as a victor in a race or combat would. Others believe that it is a diadem such as a god would wear.[16] At any rate, Beckwith is correct when he says that the crown is the eschatological reward for victory over evil.[17]

Speaking of a terrible persecution which would afflict the Church, nothing would be more in keeping with the culture of the period than to offer a crown to the overcomer. This crown

---

12 *TWNT*, V, 770.

13 Marvin Vincent, *Word Studies in the New Testament*, II, 440.

14 So Charles, *Revelation, ICC.* I, 55.

15 J. J. Reeves, "Tree of Life," *ISBE*, V, 3009.

16 I.e., a heavenly crown. So Charles, *op. cit.*, I, 58-59, and Vincent, *op. cit.*, II, 445.

17 *The Apocalypse of John*, p. 455.

is a crown that befits eternal life. With Christians this stood for the hope of immortality. The emphasis in the verse is marked: be faithful to *death* and receive the crown of *life*. Glorification is an entering into the fullness of immortal life, signified in this verse by the crown of life.

(c) Revelation 2:11 says: "He who conquers shall not be hurt by the second death." Sometimes the Scriptures emphasize a positive by stating an inconceivable negative. This is the case with this verse. The one conquering is so secure in Christ, so free from divine judgment, that he may be assuredly told that he will not be hurt (*adikeō*, to hurt, to wrong) by that last, that final, that most terrible of all judgments, the second death. The second death was a well-known rabbinic concept standing for the final judgment. Positively, the meaning of the verse is the complete, final, victorious vindication before God of those who overcome. It parallels our comments on glorification as the eschatological outcome of justification.[18]

(d) Revelation 2:17 says: "To him who conquers I will give some of the hidden manna, and I will give him a white stone, with a new name written on the stone which no one knows except him who receives it." Three blessings are awarded the overcomer: the right to eat of the hidden manna, a white stone, and a new name. There is much diversity of opinion on all three of them.

It was a rabbinic expectation that the messianic period would see the restoration of the wilderness manna. Here is a feast to which the conquerors are invited and at which they shall eat of the hidden manna.[19] To some commentators the hidden manna is the manna in the pot laid up in the ark, and to others it is not this manna but the heavenly manna as

18 Speaking of this reward Kiddle comments: "To men who daily expected the bitterest persecution — and more, the dissolution of the earth and the advent of universal judgment — no assurance could have held greater joy." *The Revelation of St. John (The Moffat New Testament Commentary)*, p. 29.

19 "Those who resist the temptation to join in the pagan banquet shall in the messianic kingdom share in the feast of the heavenly manna." Beckwith, *op. cit.*, p. 460.

such.[20] Either way the basic ideas are clear, namely, that the conquerer shall enjoy the great privilege of eating the *hidden* manna, which is a great delight because it is the manna of the messianic feast.

There is no way of ascertaining the meaning of the white stone. Some take it to mean the white stone which the athletic victor received with his name on it, not unlike the trophy given today. Others take it to mean the entrance ticket to a feast, joining with this idea the idea of the feast of the hidden manna. Charles is very strong in taking it for a powerful amulet.[21] Again, even though the precise notion cannot be settled, the idea is clear, namely, a receiving of a remarkable award for having overcome.

The new name is either the name of Christ, hidden now before the world but eschatologically revealed as the most powerful of names, or else it is a new name given to the conqueror which will fit his character and will be his eternal name. Bietenhard's position is that "he will be placed in a new station in life, in which his old guilty existence is passed. That nobody knows the new name but the one who receives it describes the unchangeability of the fellowship of every member of the Church (*Gemeinde*) with Christ."[22]

(e) Revelation 2:28 says: "And I will given him the morning star." The contrast here is between the dark days of the suffering Church and the bright day of the Church triumphant. Some take the morning star to be the new day brought in by Christ.[23] Others take it to refer to a special blessing of Christ's own personal presence, for Revelation 22:16 calls Christ the morning star.[24]

(f) Revelation 3:5 says: "He who conquers shall be clad thus in white garments, and I will not blot his name out of the book of life; I will confess his name before my Father and before his angels." Three great promises are here given to the victor.

---

20 Charles, *op. cit.*, ICC, I, 65.

21 *Ibid.*, I, 66. Both Charles and Beckwith give lists of the meaning of the white stone.

22 *TWNT*, V, 281. Also consulted for this passage in *TWNT* are IV, 941-945; IV, 466-470; III, 959-999; IV, 247-256; V, 242-283; IV, 450-456.

23 H. Lilje, *The Last Book of the Bible*, pp. 87-88.

24 Charles, *op. cit.*, I, 77.

(i) He shall wear the white garments of the glorified. White garments are heavenly, eschatological, and glorious garments.[25] Charles is of the very strong opinion that the white garments are the spiritual bodies of the redeemed.[26] The promise contained in these garments, according to Swete, is "the promise . . . of a life free from pollution, bright with celestial gladness, crowned with final victory."[27]

(ii) Again we have a positive point made by affirming an inconceivable negative. The conqueror's name shall not be blotted out of the book of life. There is a deep Old Testament and cultural background here. The theocratic kingdom had a list of names of those who would share in it, and to keep one's name in the book meant to be sure of eternal life. In other registers a man's name was scratched when he died or if he were convicted of a crime. That the name would not be blotted out speaks of the certainty, the finality, the indelibility with which the name is inscribed in the book of life. No cause can ever be found for removing the name of one of these overcomers!

(iii) Christ will confess his name before God and the angels. There is a strong, juridical meaning to the word "confess." Here in a most solemn court of God and his angels Christ will willingly confess the name of the conqueror. "To the victor Christ promises in Rev. 3:5," writes Bietenhard, "that he will not blot out his name. The validity which the name has before God rests on the fact that Christ confesses this name and thereby witnesses his fellowship with the bearer of the name before God and his angels."[28]

(g) Revelation 3:12 says: "He who conquers, I will make him a pillar in the temple of my God; never shall he go out of it, and I will write on him the name of my God, and the name of the city of my God, the New Jerusalem which comes down from my God out of heaven, and my own new name." There are two great eschatological blessings in this passage.

(i) The conqueror will be set as a pillar in the temple of God. The pillar was something of stability and beauty. This

25 *TWNT*, IV, 252.
26 *Op. cit.*, I, 82.
27 *Op. cit.*, p. 52.
28 *TWNT*, V, 281.

speaks of the permanency of the glory given the conqueror and perhaps secondly of the beautification in his glorification. Further, once being set in the temple he shall never leave it. This is stating the stability of the reward of the victor in a most emphatic manner. Philadelphia was known for its tremors which brought down the pillars of the temples. But so stable are these pillars that no shaking shall bring them down!

(ii) The conqueror will receive three names: the name of God, the name of the New Jerusalem, and the name of Christ. Basically the giving of new names goes with the new order and the new names signify full participation in the new order. The names of God and of Christ signify the vested interest of God and Christ in the conqueror and therefore his complete unassailability. The name of the New Jerusalem indicates his unalterable citizenship in that final city of God.

(h) Revelation 3:21 says: "He who conquers, I will grant him to sit with me on my throne, as I myself conquered and sat down with my Father on his throne." The blessing promised here is the blessedness of sharing in the messianic reign. It signifies the highest possible dignity in the future messianic kingdom.[29] Thus it means to share in the glory and power of Christ, to be in the exalted and heavenly condition and position of Christ.

(i) Revelation 7:15-17 says: "Therefore are they before the throne of God, and serve him day and night within his temple; and he who sits upon the throne will shelter them with his presence. They shall hunger no more, neither thirst any more; the sun shall not strike them, nor any scorching heat. For the Lamb in the midst of the throne will be their shepherd, and he will guide them to springs of living water; and God will wipe away every tear from their eyes."

These words are said of the servants of God, the great multitude which came out of the great tribulation and have washed their robes and made them white in the blood of the Lamb. Nine remarkable blessings of the glorious state of these servants of the Lord are described.

(i) They are before the throne of God. The reason is (*dia touto*) that they have washed their robes in the blood of the

29 Beckwith, *op. cit.*, p. 491.

Lamb. This qualifies them to stand in the very presence of God without fear, without shame, without tremor and in full acceptance by the divine majesty. This is yet another time that the full, final, complete vindication of the believer in the end-time is spoken of.

(ii) They serve God day and night in his temple. The covenantal people of God are to render such service to God. In the course of Israel's history this service was limited to the tribe of Levi. Here we have the priestly rights of the total people of God, as by their service they exhibit their perfect communion with God. Furthermore, there is no interruption in this divine service. That which the Levitical priests stood for, in terms of service and communion with God, is perfectly realized by the redeemed in heaven as pictured in this passage.

(iii) They shall be sheltered by the presence of God. Charles thinks that this means that the Shekinah Glory will abide on the saints.[30] The passage looks back to two things. It looks back to the terrible days of persecution when it seemed as if the persecuted were unprotected and therefore like sheep led to the slaughter (Rom. 8:36). And it looks back either to the Shekinah Glory or to the protecting pillar of fire by day and cloud by night of the exodus experience. Never again will these people undergo torment. They now have the supreme or maximum protection, the protection of the living God himself.

(iv) They shall hunger no more. Times of persecution can be times of starvation. In their persecution they might have fled without provisions. Like those mentioned in Hebrews 11:37, they might have wandered about in skins of sheep and goats, destitute, afflicted and ill-treated. Perhaps they lay famished in a prison. But such terrible days are forever over. What is more, all that these people hungered for — Matthew 5:6! — is satisfied!

(v) They shall thirst no more. Terrible thirst, more terrible than hunger, could also have been the fate of these Christians. Again it might have been a dungeon experience, or it might have been a flight into the barren desert. But these had known the agonies of thirst. And like they hungered they had

30 *Op. cit.*, I, 215.

also thirsted for something. Never again shall these people know thirst, and all that their souls spiritually thirsted for shall be more than fulfilled.

(vi) They shall not be struck by the sun nor any scorching heat. Again the background is the terrible days of persecution. To be caught without provision under a burning sun is a frightful experience. The gentle sun of spring becomes a tyrant of a furnace in the summer time. In flight these martyrs knew the burning of the sun. They also might have been staked out in the sun to suffer its agonizing heat. But all of this is now past. They are forever free from any such torment.

(vii) The Lamb will be their shepherd. The writer now starts a contrast in another direction. Once these Christians were at the mercy of their tormentors. Like Peter they were carried where they did not wish to go (John 21:18). They went many places and did many things contrary to their wills. But now they are in the hands of the Lamb. They shall be led by God's dear Son and not by tormentors.

(viii) He will guide them to springs of living water. Living water is water that eternally gushes up, in contrast to the well that becomes dry or the pool that becomes a muddy hole. It was the most valuable source of water supply that one could have. The Lamb will guide these Christians to this kind of water supply. Never again will they know the brackish pool or the muddied hole or the stagnant marsh. But there is something more here. There is the pastoral picture of shepherd and contented sheep. Hence the eternal reward of these Christians will be eternal felicity in the presence of Christ. It will be eternal joy which knows no staleness, repetition or satiation.

(ix) God shall wipe away every tear from their eyes. Tribulation produces tears. These Christians might have seen fellow Christians put to death; they might have seen their own flesh tortured for Christ's sake; they might have languished in some prison seemingly forgotten or intentionally ignored. Thus when they arrive in heaven they arrive with tears of persecution and suffering in their eyes. Like a tenderhearted, devoted Father, God shall wipe each tear out of their eyes with the eternal consolations of glory itself. Nothing else could dry up such eyes. And never again shall anything happen to them that shall cause them to cry, but on the contrary they shall be eternally delighted with the joys of an everlasting glorification.

(j) Revelation 19:8 says: "It was granted to her to be clothed with fine linen, bright and pure — for the fine linen is the righteous deeds of the saints." The context of this passage is the speech made by the great multitude. The time of the marriage of the Lamb has come. The bride is ready and her garment is described. It is a simple garment of white linen, standing in marked contrast to the garments of the great harlot. Linen was expensive garment used particularly by priests and by royalty. Two adjectives are used to describe it in this passage. The garment was bright (*lampros*). This means a shimmering whiteness.[31] In Revelation the white shimmering garment is the garment of glorification. Secondly, it is a pure (*katharos*) garment. The priests who wore white linen attempted to keep their garments meticulously clean. The bride has not only a beautiful white linen garment but it is spotless. This notion of purity is strongly eschatological, for the emphasis on purity as the quality of the New Jerusalem is sustained. Purity is that which is proper and correct for holy uses and for commerce with God.[32]

Then there is added the explanatory sentence that fine linen is the righteous deeds of the saints. This is not to indicate any kind of salvation by works. There is first of all a note of grace in the verse itself: the garments are *granted* her. The real purport is to show that the saints have an inner beauty which corresponds to their external glorification. Some writers prefer to say that the fine linen is the righteousness of the saints, but the Greek will not allow it. *Dikaiōma* are righteous deeds, not righteousness. The contrast here is between the faithful believers who have been true to God, and those who followed the false prophet, or the false beast, or the great whore. In this connection the righteous deeds of the saints are their fine linen.

(k) Revelation 21:3-5 says: "And I heard a great voice from the throne saying, 'Behold, the dwelling of God is with men.

31 *TWNT*, IV, 27.
32 *TWNT*, III, 427.

He will dwell with them, and they shall be his people, and God himself will be with them; he will wipe away every tear from their eyes, and death shall be no more, neither shall there be mourning nor crying nor pain any more, for the former things have passed away.' "

This passage is in immediate connection with the vision of the new heaven, the new earth, and the New Jerusalem coming down out of heaven adorned as a bride for her groom. The great voice describes the blessedness of those who will be in the New Jerusalem.

(i) The first great blessing is the intimate association of God with the redeemed. The dwelling of God, the New Jerusalem, comes down to the new earth and there is inhabited by God and the redeemed. The New Jerusalem shall be the dwelling of God *then* just as heaven is represented as his dwelling *now*. In fulfillment of so many prophetic passages, God will be God *present* with man. The tabernacle and temple were both typical and prophetic of this ultimate eternal realization. All that those two structures typified in terms of the *presence* of God with his people is now perfectly, completely, gloriously realized.

(ii) God will wipe away every tear. This expression has already been commented upon in another connection. But the occurrence of this expression in this place gives it a wider importance. *It speaks of the tears of human existence.* The human race has cried over a thousand things. One is reminded of Job 5:7 — "But man is born to trouble as the sparks fly upward." The history of the human race is the history of tragedy upon tragedy, calamity upon calamity, heartache upon heartache, plague upon plague, disappointment upon disappointment, evil upon evil. When the curtain finally drops upon the course of human history it will close upon a humanity filled with far more tears than joy, with far more heartaches than happiness. *God's own people have had their share of heartache and tears.* Eternity cannot begin until the tears of the redeemed are wiped away, i.e., until all that has hurt, wounded, and cut has been mollified by the divine benevolence. The directness of the expression is most tender: *God himself shall wipe away every tear!* This is a task too personal, a care too deep to trust to anybody but himself. The positive side of the wiping away of all tears is entering into a state of perfect, eternal felicity.

(iii) Death shall be no more. Can a more gladsome word be said to humanity than this? Nothing has pursued humanity more relentlessly and more successfully than death. The word itself stands for a thousand heartaches and a million miseries. No happy union has been formed of friends or family or associates that has not finally been dissolved by death. Sometimes it has been the rough hand of accident; other times it has been the unexpected swift course of disease; other times it has been the exhausting slow course of disease. The sun never sets without some family gathering at the graveside of a loved one with all the uncontrollable feelings, the massive lump in the throat, the torrent of tears, the horrible vacant feeling, that dreadful vacuum created by the loss of a loved one.

Death has also worked its dreary work in the history of the Christian Church. It silenced the voice of a Spurgeon as it stilled the pen of Augustine. It put more than one missionary into an early grave. It eventually breaks the strength of the most valiant. It brings low the worthy pastor, the dedicated Christian scholar, the seemingly tireless Christian layworker.

Now comes the great announcement! Death shall be no more! It has claimed its last victim. The final funeral has been held. In Emmanuel's land there shall be no funeral parlors or graveyards. There shall only be the glorious triumph of life, so glorious and so triumphant that death shall be no more!

(iv) There shall be no more mourning. The Scriptures oppose laughter to mourning (Luke 6:25, Jas. 4:9). In the New Testament men mourn over their sins (Matt. 5:4), over the departed groom (Matt. 9:5), over the crucified Saviour (Mark 16:10), and over the sinning brother (II Cor. 12:21). To these mournings many other thousands may be added. The parent mourns over the wayward life of the son or daughter. A nation has mourned at a time of national catastrophe — the loss of a leader, the loss of a great battle, the loss from a storm or earthquake or fire.

Whatever the cause of mourning, from causes of human existence or from causes of spiritual concern, the days of mourning are ended when the New Jerusalem comes down from heaven. *Nothing shall happen in its eternal history that shall ever cause one of the redeemed to mourn. Nothing in the past shall rise up and in its remembrance cause one of the redeemed to mourn.* If laughter is the antonym of mourning then heaven shall be filled with the ring of eternal laughter.

(v) There shall be no more crying (*kraugē*). In most of the New Testament passages in which this word is used (as verb and as noun) it means to shout, to cry aloud. Only in two references does it refer to weeping. One is the passage before us and the other is Hebrews 5:7, which speaks of the prayers and supplications made by Christ with *loud shouts* and tears. This kind of crying is not, then, ordinary weeping but that violent sound wrenched from the throat by some most painful experience. It is the weeping inspired by grief and anxiety. It is the broken heart, the embittered heart, the frustrated heart, the disappointed heart that cries. And what makes it cry? All of those things of life that can cause agony. And Christians, too, have tasted of these agonies. In fact, due to their commitment to Christ and involvement with the ongoing of the gospel they have experienced more agonies than the unregenerate.

But again the glad word comes. Nothing that has caused agony shall ever again cause the human throat to burst forth in an agonizing cry. And nothing shall ever happen in the Eternal City that shall cause a saint to cry. Those that mourn shall be comforted, and those, too, who have cried shall be comforted, and that with the eternal consolations of the New Jerusalem.

(vi) There shall be no more pain (*ponos*). How the human race has suffered from pain. Not a second of the clock ticks without millions of human beings enduring pain. Some of it is emotional or mental, some of it is spiritual, but most of it is physical. There is the pounding pain of the headache, the sharp pain of a toothache, the slow gnawing pain of some deep organic disorder. There is the relentless pain from arthritis and the merciless pain of cancer. Although perhaps a few persons have gone through life virtually free from pain, most of the millions of the earth have suffered not one pain but many pains. Even though we know that pain is a signal from the body that something is wrong, this knowledge makes the pain no easier to bear. And what pains might be ahead of us from atomic radiation?

But when the New Jerusalem comes into being pain has had its last day. The aching tooth has been a pocket of fire for the last time. The last cancer will have brought its hapless victim to the grave. The deep-seated aches of the bones are forever gone. Pain shall be no more! In our glorified body we shall be free from every disease. Nothing, absolutely nothing, can exist in the New Jerusalem to cause pain. Upon the resurrection body shall rest the blush of eternal youth, with its wonderful gift of eternal health.

In a summary statement John says that the former things have passed away. The former things are the things of the old heaven, the old earth, the old existence. This is the existence of hunger and thirst, of pain and death. But that order is gone forever. *All things are made new!* Apocalyptically new! Messianically new! Eschatologically new! In this eternal newness there is no more room for tears or death or mourning or crying or pain. *These things have all passed away* and they are replaced by the eternal joys of the New Jerusalem.

(1) Revelation 22:1-5 says: "Then he showed me the river of the water of life, bright as crystal, flowing from the throne of God and of the Lamb through the middle of the street of the city; also, on either side of the river, the tree of life with its twelve kinds of fruit, yielding its fruit each month; and the leaves of the tree were for the healing of the nations. There shall no more be anything accursed, but the throne of God and of the Lamb shall be in it, and his servants shall worship him; they shall see his face, and his name shall be on their foreheads. And night shall be no more; they need no light of lamp or sun, for the Lord God will be their light, and they shall reign for ever and ever."

In these words the final glorification and felicity of the redeemed are set forth. There are eight great signs of blessedness in this passage.

(i) The first glorious blessing is the river of life. In this passage is brought together the rivers of Eden and the river of the eschatological vision of Ezekiel, but in an exalted and advanced representation.[33] Four things are said of this river: (a) It arises from the throne of God and the Lamb. This is the strongest conjunction in the book of Revelation of God and the Lamb. From God and the Lamb is the source of the river of life, i.e., the source of all the blessedness the river of life stands for. The throne is the center of importance in the new Jerusalem and this river of life flows directly out of the throne. (b) It is living water. This harks back to the issues of life and death that existed in Adam's probation. Here in the New Jerusalem there is no probation. *There is only life!* And it is there in such abundance that its only fit symbol is a perpetually flowing river of living waters! (c) It is pure water. It is described as being bright as crystal. This expresses the heavenliness and paradisaical character of the water[34] and the glorious nature of all things in heaven. Not one fleck of dirt is in this water, but it shines like a jewel. (d) As a river it represents the endless source of life, the inexhaustibility of the source of life for the glorified saints in the New Jerusalem.

(ii) Planted alongside the river are twelve trees, spoken of collectively as the tree of life. Apparently the water from the river is not directly drunk, but its virtue is implanted into the trees and derived from eating the fruit and the leaves of the trees. Each month of the year the trees bear fruit. Again in this picture we have elements from both Genesis and Ezekiel.

Just as with the river, two things stand out in this representation. The first is the matter of life. The fruit of the tree gives immortal life and the leaves of the tree are for the healing of the nations; no sickness — mental, emotional, moral, social — can ever emerge in the New Jerusalem. The second is the idea of fullness. This is represented by the tree of life now being twelve trees and bearing fruit each month of the

33 *TWNT*, VI, 605.
34 *TWNT*, IV, 27.

year. Here is the overpowering representation of the victory of life over death.

(iii) The absolute purity of the city is stressed. Negatively it is stated that no accursed thing or person is in the city. Not one vestige, not one trace, not one iota of the fearful and awful history of sin carries over into the New Jerusalem. Not even the shadow of a moral flaw can be found there. Positively it is affirmed that the throne of God and the Lamb is there. This throne could only rest in a place of perfection, of indefectable purity, of unchallenged holiness. Thus the victory of righteousness will be absolutely absolute in the New Jerusalem.

(iv) The servants of God and the Lamb shall be engaged in perpetual worship. The chief end of man is to glorify God, and worship is the supreme means of glorifying God. It would be unthinkable for the redeemed creature to be before God and not worship him. Therefore they shall worship him continually in a worship that is perfect in its execution and perfection in its reception by the divine majesty. All that the human tongue has not been able to say or sing in *this* life shall be gloriously overcome in *that* life and we shall praise him as he ought to be praised.

(v) His servants shall see his face. Seeing the face of an oriental king was a great privilege, and one of the supreme penalties of a condemned man was that he could not see the face of the king. In *this* life we know God indirectly, in terms of signs, by faith and not by sight. But in our state of glorification our knowledge of God shall be face to face! Words completely fail to convey the glory, the wonder, the beauty, the passion, and the ecstasy of seeing him face to face.

(vi) The redeemed shall have the name of God on their foreheads. All through the book of Revelation the mark on the forehead is laden with significance, either of great evil or great blessing. It of course represents *a sealing*. The redeemed as glorified are sealed eternally with the name of God. It also is a great revelation of grace and love. God does not readily share his name or his glory. Yet he gives the glorified ones the unspeakable privilege of having his name on their foreheads. It means to be under the total ownership, the total protectorship of God. No judgment can ever arise that can call in question the status of one who has the name of God upon his forehead.

(vii) The glory of God is the illumination of the city. The passage of night into day and day into night belongs to the old order. There will be no night there, for the night is part of the old order. The need of the lamp by night and the sun by day belongs to the old order. But in the new order, the eschatological order, the order of glorification, God's glory is the light of the New Jerusalem. Feel the wonderful imagery here. The glorified shall walk and live in the light provided by the glory of God!

(viii) The curtain of revelation drops with the final vision of glorification. The glorified shall reign for ever and ever. It is a *reign!* That is, it is a condition of complete glorification. It is a condition of perfect sharing in the wonder of God. And it is *eternal.* It will last for ever and ever. And thus the vision ends with the redeemed in a state of eternal glory living through age after age of eternity reigning with God and the Lamb, knowing an existence free from all pain, death, and mourning, and knowing an existence only of happiness, bliss, joy, and glory without surcease.

SELECT BIBLIOGRAPHY

Abrahams, I. *The Glory of God.* Oxford: Oxford University Press, 1925.

Althaus, Paul. *Die christliche Wahrheit.* Fifth edition. Gütersloh: Carl Bertelmann, Verlag, 1959.

Berquist, Millard. "The Meaning of *Doxa* in the Epistles of Paul." Louisville: Southern Baptist Seminary; unpublished doctoral dissertation, 1941.

Cullmann, Oscar. *Immortality of the Soul or Resurrection of the Dead?* London: The Epworth Press, 1958.

Davies, J. G. *He Ascended into Heaven.* New York: Association Press, 1958.

De Young, J. C. *Jerusalem in the New Testament.* Kampen: J. H. Kok, 1960.

Gall, F. *Die Herrlichkeit Gottes.* Giessen: J. Ricker'sche Verlag-Buchhandlung, 1900.

Jacob, Edmund. *Theology of the Old Testament.* New York: Harpers, 1958.

Johnson, A. R. *The One and the Many in the Israelite Conception of God.* Second edition. Cardiff: University of Wales Press, 1961.

Kittel, Helmuth. *Die Herrlichkeit Gottes.* Giessen: Verlag von Alfred Topelmann, 1934.

Köhler, Ludwig. *Old Testament Theology.* Philadelphia: Westminster Press, 1957.

Owen, D.R.G. *Body and Soul.* Philadelphia: The Westminster Press, 1956.

Prenter, Regin. *Schöpfung und Erlösung.* Göttingen: Vandenhoeck and Ruprecht, 1960.

Pythian-Adams, J. G. *The People and the Presence.* New York: Oxford University Press, 1942.

Robinson, J. A. T. *The Body.* Chicago: Henry Regnery Co., 1952.

Rowley, H. H. *The Re-Discovery of the Old Testament.* Philadelphia: The Westminster Press, 1946.

Rust, E. C. *Nature and Man in Biblical Thought.* London: Lutterworth Press, 1953.

Simon, Ulrich. *Heaven in the Christian Tradition.* New York: Harpers, 1958.

Staufer, E. *New Testament Theology.* New York: The Macmillan Co., 1955.

Taylor, A. E. *The Christian Hope of Immortality.* New York: The Macmillan Co., 1947.

Vriezen, Th. *An Outline of Old Testament Theology.* Boston: C. T. Branford, 1958.

INDEX OF SCRIPTURES

144 INDEX OF SCRIPTURES

INDEX OF AUTHORS

INDEX OF SUBJECTS